YORK

D0514098

FRANKENSTEIN

MARY SHELLEY

NOTES BY ALEXANDER FAIRBAIRN-DIXON

 Longman

The right of Alexander Fairbairn-Dixon to be identified as Author of
this Work has been asserted by him in accordance with the
Copyright, Designs and Patents Act 1988

YORK PRESS
322 Old Brompton Road, London SW5 9JH

PEARSON EDUCATION LIMITED
Edinburgh Gate, Harlow,
Essex CM20 2JE, United Kingdom
Associated companies, branches and representatives throughout the world

First published 1999
This new and fully revised edition first published 2003
Third impression 2004

10 9 8 7 6 5 4 3

ISBN 0-582-77267-2

Designed by Michelle Cannatella
Illustrated by Neil Evans
Typeset by Pantek Arts Ltd, Maidstone, Kent
Produced by Pearson Education Asia Limited, Hong Kong

CONTENTS

PREFACE

York Notes are designed to give you a broader perspective on works of literature studied at GCSE and equivalent levels. With examination requirements changing in the twenty-first century, we have made a number of significant changes to this new series. We continue to help students to reach their own interpretations of the text but York Notes now have important extra-value new features.

You will discover that York Notes are genuinely interactive. The new **Checkpoint** features make sure that you can test your knowledge and broaden your understanding. You will also be directed to excellent websites, books and films where you can follow up ideas for yourself.

The **Resources** section has been updated and an entirely new section has been devoted to how to improve your grade. Careful reading and application of the principles laid out in the Resources section guarantee improved performance.

The **Detailed summaries** include an easy-to-follow skeleton structure of the story-line, while the section on **Language and style** has been extended to offer an in-depth discussion of the writer's techniques.

The Contents page shows the structure of this study guide. However, there is no need to read from the beginning to the end as you would with a novel, play or poem. Use the Notes in the way that suits you. Our aim is to help you with your understanding of the work, not to dictate how you should learn.

Our authors are practising English teachers and examiners who have used their experience to offer a whole range of **Examiner's secrets** – useful hints to encourage exam success.

The General Editor of this series is John Polley, Senior GCSE Examiner and former Head of English at Harrow Way Community School, Andover.

The author of these Notes is Alexander Fairbairn-Dixon, who graduated from the University of East Anglia with a first class degree in English literature. He has worked as the English Co-ordinator at a college in Teeside.

The text used in these Notes is the Penguin Popular Classics edition of *Frankenstein* (1818; revised 1831) published in 1994.

PART ONE

INTRODUCTION

HOW TO STUDY A NOVEL

A novelist starts with a story that examines a situation and the actions of particular characters. Remember that authors are not photographers, and that a novel never resembles real life exactly. Ultimately, a novel represents a view of the world that has been created in the author's imagination.

There are six features of a novel:

1 THE STORY: this is the series of events, deliberately organised by the writer to test the characters

2 THE CHARACTERS: the people who have to respond to the events of the story. Since they are human, they can be good or bad, clever or stupid, likeable or detestable, etc. They may change too!

3 THE VIEWPOINT/VOICE: who is telling the story. The viewpoint may come from one of the characters, or from an omniscient (all-seeing) narrator, which allows the novelist to write about the perspectives of all the characters

4 THE THEMES: these are the underlying messages, or meanings, of the novel

5 THE SETTING: this concerns the time and place that the author has chosen for the story

6 THE LANGUAGE AND STYLE: these are the words that the author has used to influence our understanding of the novel

To arrive at the fullest understanding of a novel, you need to read it several times. In this way, you can see how all the choices the author has made add up to a particular view of life, and develop your own ideas about it.

The purpose of these York Notes is to help you understand what the novel is about and to enable you to make your own interpretation. Do not expect the study of a novel to be neat and easy: novels are chosen for examination purposes, not written for them!

? DID YOU KNOW?
The inspiration for *Frankenstein* came from 'a half-waking nightmare'.

AUTHOR – LIFE AND WORKS

1756 Birth of William Godwin, political writer, Mary's future father

1759 Birth of Mary Wollstonecraft, the first feminist, Mary's future mother

1792 Birth of Percy Bysshe Shelley, Mary's future husband

1797 William marries Mary who is pregnant by him. Mary Godwin Wollstonecraft is born in London, her mother dying within a matter of days

1801 Mary's father remarries

1811 Shelley expelled from Oxford and elopes to Scotland with 16-year-old Harriet Westbrook, whom he later marries

1812–14 Mary stays with father's friends in Scotland

1814 Mary elopes to France with Percy Bysshe Shelley

1815 Mary gives birth to a child who dies twelve days later

1816 Shelley's wife, Harriet, drowns herself. Mary marries Shelley. They spend time with Byron at Lake Geneva, where Mary writes *Frankenstein*

1818 The Shelleys leave England for Italy, *Frankenstein* published

1819 Mary begins *Mathilda*

1822 Percy Shelley drowns

1823 Mary returns to live in England; *Valperga* a romance set in Italy published

1826 *The Last Man* a novel set in the 21st century is published

1831 Revised version of *Frankenstein*

1835 Mary's *Ladore* tells the story of Shelley's first marriage

1837 *Falkner,* her last novel, published

1844 *Rambles in Germany and Italy*

1851 Mary Shelley dies

CONTEXT

1770–74 Births of three poets: William Wordsworth, Samuel Taylor Coleridge, Robert Southey

1788 French Revolution begins; birth of Lord Byron, poet

1790 Wordsworth on walking tour of France and sympathetic to revolutionaries

1793 William Godwin's writing brings him the friendship of Coleridge, Wordsworth, Southey and Shelley

1798 Publication of Coleridge's *Rime of the Ancient Mariner*

1800 Alessandro Volta invents electric battery

1802 Luigi Galvani, in experiments with frogs, believes he has discovered electricity present in human limbs

1811–14 Shelley lives in Lake District, meeting Southey, and in Lynmouth, meeting Coleridge

1813 Southey becomes Poet Laureate

1815 Napoleon becomes emperor and is defeated at Waterloo

1816 Jane Austen's *Emma* is published; invention of wooden stethoscope

1818 First (unsuccessful) blood transfusions at Guy's hospital, London

1820 George III dies, George IV succeeds

1823 Byron dies of marsh fever in the Greek struggle for independence

1833 Slavery is abolished

1834 Coleridge dies

1843 Death of Southey; Wordsworth becomes Poet Laureate

1850 Death of Wordsworth

SETTING AND BACKGROUND

THE LIFE OF MARY SHELLEY

Mary Shelley was only nineteen years old when she completed her novel *Frankenstein*. Since then her monster has become so popular that in the twenty-first century, we see him in films, advertisements, comics and even computer games.

How is it then that the young Mary Shelley wrote a book that has become more famous than any other work of Romantic literature and, indeed, herself? Her unconventional life and upbringing might give us a clue.

Parents and early years

Mary grew up in a cultured environment and became an avid reader. Although Godwin was an emotionally distant father, he was a good teacher and Mary had free access to her father's extensive library and literary connections: aged four she and her stepsister, Claire Clairmont, hid behind the sofa out of fear when the great Romantic poet, Samuel Taylor Coleridge recited *The Rime of the Ancient Mariner*.

1812–22 Romance and Tragedy

This period of Mary's life is characterised by adventure and death. Between 1812 and 1814 she stayed with Godwin's acquaintances, the Baxters, in Scotland. These sublime surroundings aroused her and she began to write. On returning home (aged sixteen) she was to find a new visitor, the young poet Percy Shelley, who, although recently married, was to become her future husband. He was a handsome young man with flaming auburn hair, whose wild emotions, energetic imagination and intense excitement for nature, the supernatural and science (see below) make him a fascinating poet to read. It was not long before they fell in love.

In July 1814 they eloped to the continent with Claire. However, both of their fathers were enraged by the illicitness of the affair and effectively disowned them. Pursued by Shelley's creditors on returning to England, they left for Switzerland in 1816 where they met the poet Lord Byron, at whose villa Mary started *Frankenstein*.

DID YOU KNOW?

Mary's father was a philosopher, anarchist, atheist, novelist, and an ex-minister of religion.

Worse was to follow: in 1816 Mary's half-sister committed suicide, and Percy Shelley's wife drowned herself. Although this circumstance enabled Mary to marry Percy, they were never forgiven by their fathers. Mary's second child, William, died at the age of three. And Percy Shelley himself drowned in 1822. By 1824, with the death of Lord Byron, Mary found herself isolated and alone.

1824–51 Writing and motherhood

Her friends and family gone, Mary devoted her time during this period to the upbringing of her only surviving child, Percy Florence Shelley, and writing for journals and magazines. She also published the second revised version of *Frankenstein* in 1831, and wrote the futuristic novel *The Last Man*. Mary Shelley died at the age of fifty-three in 1851.

SOCIAL MONSTERS

When Shelley was writing *Frankenstein*, she was reading *Emile* by a famous French philosopher, Jean-Jacques Rousseau, whose ideas inspired the French Revolution. In this book he argues that man's nature is harmless but that men are made evil by society. Men become 'monsters' by the way they are treated. However, he says that 'a man abandoned to himself in the midst of other men from birth would be the most disfigured of all'. This debate is at the heart of the book: the monster is born good but becomes wicked because people abuse and reject him. Worst of all, his creator, Victor Frankenstein, refuses to grant him his natural rights of Freedom, Equality and Fraternity.

Victor Frankenstein grows up in the Swiss city of Geneva, and it was here that Mary Shelley started to write her novel. During the summer of 1816 Percy, Mary and her stepsister Claire visited Lord Byron at the Villa Diodati, from where they could see the majestic Alps. Here they also met 'Monk' Lewis, famed for his supernatural stories, and Dr Polidori, Byron's young physician. The group formed a habit of talking into the early hours, and one night Byron read aloud some ghost stories from a book called *Fantasmagoriana*. He challenged the gathering to a ghost story competition. This set the Gothic tone for Mary's novel.

CHECK THE FILM

The first film of the book was made in 1909 and starred Charles Ogle.

DID YOU KNOW?

The first **Gothic novel** was *The Castle of Otranto* (1764) by Horace Walpole.

Mary was clearly excited by the sublime nature of the scenery; she wrote: 'The thunder storms that visit us are grander and more terrific than I have ever seen before. We watch them approach from the opposite side of the lake, observing the lightning play among the clouds in various parts of the heavens, and dart in jagged figures upon the piny heights.'

Climbing the Alps, she saw the *Mer de Glace* (the sea of ice) near Mont Blanc: the desolate scene where Frankenstein and his monster first meet (pp. 93–5).

MYTHS AND LEGENDS

Mary Shelley alludes to many myths in the course of *Frankenstein*.

Prometheus

There are two versions of the Prometheus myth. In the Greek version he is a rebel who steals fire from the ruler of the gods, Zeus, and a friend to humanity because he gives them 'the gift of fire' but is then eternally punished by Zeus. In the Latin version, Prometheus creates man from clay and water. Victor is a 'Modern Prometheus' because he rebels against the laws of nature by making an unnatural man because it would be of 'benefit to mankind' and he is punished for his efforts by his creation.

 DID YOU KNOW?
Percy Bysshe Shelley wrote a famous drama called *Prometheus Unbound* in 1818–19.

Faustus (or Faust)

Dr Faustus is an academic who rejects normal pursuits for magic because he wants to know the secrets of the universe. He sells his soul to Satan in exchange for this knowledge but does not know what to do with his power. Tormented by the deal, he eventually perishes in hell. Similarly, Frankenstein relinquishes his family for the pursuit of secret knowledge, and, working in isolation, creates a creature that he abandons. The monster revenges himself, like a devil, by destroying Victor's family and friends.

 DID YOU KNOW?
Christopher Marlowe, a contemporary of Shakespeare, and another great Romantic writer, Goethe, both wrote plays about Faust.

The Fall of Man

Adam and Eve in the Book of Genesis are forbidden by God to eat from the tree of knowledge. Tempted by Satan, they rebel. They become aware of their own sexuality, and are eventually banished from the Garden of Eden. Similarly, Victor's childhood is like paradise but he is seduced by knowledge in adulthood. He rebels by creating an unnatural man. The monster also becomes aware of his own 'fallen' state when he sees his own reflection.

Paradise Lost

This is an epic poem written by John Milton in the 1660s. It tells the story of how Satan was banished from heaven by God for leading a rebellion. Satan, unable to accept his fall into hell, decides to revenge himself by seducing Adam and Eve into evil and disobedience.

These references are sustained and add a whole new pattern of meaning to the novel.

PASSIONATE LITERATURE

Frankenstein is often seen as a **Romantic** novel. Romanticism focuses on the expression of the imagination, exalted and intense feelings, visionary states of mind, and the sublime power of nature. Romantics believed that art should have themes of great magnitude which could arouse emotional exhilaration in the audience.

The Romantics were influenced by philosophers of the Enlightenment, particularly those who either argued for individual liberty or explored the sublime.

 DID YOU KNOW?

Other writers influenced by the Gothic novel are the Brontë sisters and the American Edgar Allan Poe.

An offshoot of **Romanticism** was the **Gothic** novel which began in 1764 with Horace Walpole's dream-induced *The Castle of Otranto*. *Frankenstein* therefore belongs to the tradition of fantasy rather than realism. The uncanny events, stormy and dark settings, satanic imagery, and themes of revenge and pursuit are some of its Gothic features.

SECRETS OF SCIENCE

Mary Shelley lived at a time of rapid progress in the sciences. One of the central preoccupations was the potential of electricity. In 1802 Galvani showed that running a current through the legs of frogs produced a twitch, and was thought to engender life. And, in 1803, Aldini attached a battery to the corpse of a criminal: 'The jaw of the deceased began to quiver, the adjoining muscles were horribly contorted, and one eye was actually opened … the right hand was raised and clenched, and the legs and thighs set in motion.'

These discoveries were discussed at Byron's villa. (Percy Shelley was known to have electrocuted himself until his hair stood on end and he possessed electro-magnetic kites which could bring down lightning in the event of a storm.)

DID YOU KNOW?

Mary Shelley said she named Frankenstein after the American politician Benjamin Franklin (1706–90) who famously used a kite to demonstrate the power of electricity.

Now, take a break!

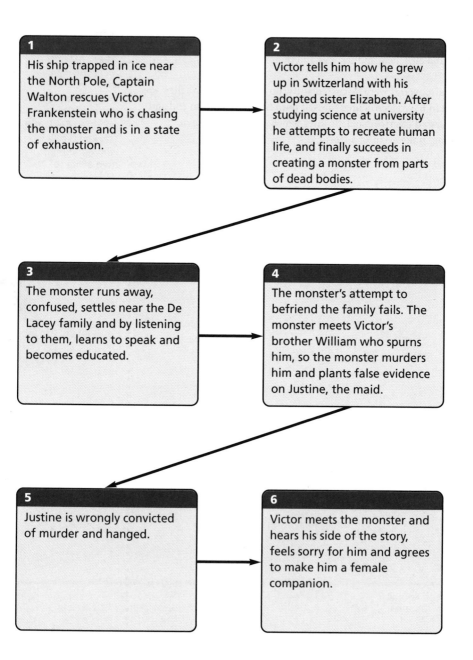

1

His ship trapped in ice near the North Pole, Captain Walton rescues Victor Frankenstein who is chasing the monster and is in a state of exhaustion.

2

Victor tells him how he grew up in Switzerland with his adopted sister Elizabeth. After studying science at university he attempts to recreate human life, and finally succeeds in creating a monster from parts of dead bodies.

3

The monster runs away, confused, settles near the De Lacey family and by listening to them, learns to speak and becomes educated.

4

The monster's attempt to befriend the family fails. The monster meets Victor's brother William who spurns him, so the monster murders him and plants false evidence on Justine, the maid.

5

Justine is wrongly convicted of murder and hanged.

6

Victor meets the monster and hears his side of the story, feels sorry for him and agrees to make him a female companion.

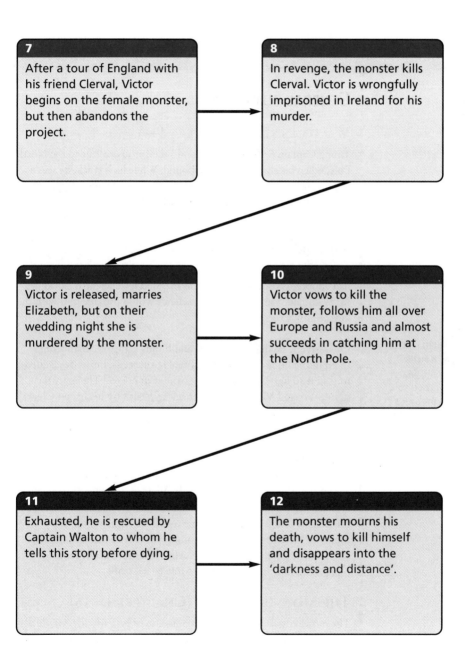

7
After a tour of England with his friend Clerval, Victor begins on the female monster, but then abandons the project.

8
In revenge, the monster kills Clerval. Victor is wrongfully imprisoned in Ireland for his murder.

9
Victor is released, marries Elizabeth, but on their wedding night she is murdered by the monster.

10
Victor vows to kill the monster, follows him all over Europe and Russia and almost succeeds in catching him at the North Pole.

11
Exhausted, he is rescued by Captain Walton to whom he tells this story before dying.

12
The monster mourns his death, vows to kill himself and disappears into the 'darkness and distance'.

PART TWO

SUMMARIES

GENERAL SUMMARY

WALTON'S STORY (LETTERS 1–4)

Young Captain Robert Walton is on a dangerous voyage to the North Pole, when his ship becomes ice bound. While he is stuck, he sees a gigantic being on a sledge travelling at great speed who disappears into the fog. He then discovers Victor Frankenstein on the brink of death. Walton looks after him and Frankenstein tells him his story.

VICTOR'S STORY (CHAPTERS 1–10)

Victor grew up with an orphan named Elizabeth whom his mother had adopted. At university he was inspired by a scientist called M. Waldman. Victor hoped that science would provide him with the key of how to create life itself.

Obsessively, he digs up corpses and builds a gigantic man from them in the hope of giving him life. He succeeds, but is devastated to find it so ugly, and runs away from it in horror. The monster disappears and Victor is nursed back to health by his friend Clerval.

However, he receives a letter from his father telling him that his youngest brother, William, has been murdered. Victor quickly journeys home to Geneva. On the way, he sees the monster amidst the Alps, and becomes convinced that the monster is William's murderer. When he meets his family, Victor learns that Justine, their servant, has been accused of the murder. Justine falsely confesses to the murder and is hanged. Unable to tell his family about the monster, Victor spends his time alone. He travels into the Alps where he meets the monster. He wants to kill him. The monster reproaches him and asks him to listen to his story.

THE MONSTER'S STORY (CHAPTERS 11–16)

The monster tells him about the confusion of his early life. Gradually, he learns about the world. On wandering into a village he is attacked and flees. In hiding he observes the daily life of a poor family called the De Laceys. He is moved by the kindness the son and daughter

DID YOU KNOW?

As a child, Mary Shelley used to sit by her mother's grave and write.

show towards their old, blind father. When a young Arabian arrives, the son teaches her his language and the monster learns it by listening. When the blind man is alone, the monster introduces himself. The family returns. Seeing the monster, the son batters him. In anguish, the monster decides to seek out his creator. On the way he saves a young girl from drowning but is shot by a peasant. Later, he tries to befriend a young boy, William, but William rejects him and also fatally reveals that he is a Frankenstein. In revenge for his miseries, the monster strangles him. He takes a portrait from his neck and places it within the dress of a girl who is sleeping – Justine. Finally, the monster explains that his misery and loneliness has made him act badly. He asks Victor to create a female monster for him.

VICTOR'S STORY CONTINUES (CHAPTERS 17–24)

Victor finally agrees to do so. His father proposes that Victor marry Elizabeth. Victor agrees to do so after he has taken a tour of England, on which he is accompanied by Clerval. In the Orkney islands Victor parts with his friend and hires a hut, so that he can make the female monster. But when he sees the monster at the window, in a fury, he tears the half-finished female creature to pieces. The monster, in despair, leaves him with the words, 'I shall be with you on your wedding night!'

The monster murders Clerval and makes it look as though Victor was the murderer. Victor spends time in prison in a state of madness. Eventually, he is proved innocent. He marries Elizabeth. On their honeymoon, while Victor is out looking for the monster, he kills Elizabeth. Victor's father dies when he hears the news. Utterly alone, Victor decides to seek out the monster and kill him. He chases him and almost manages to kill him near the North Pole. Victor finds himself sinking when Walton's ship passes by and rescues him.

WALTON'S STORY CONTINUES (THE FINAL LETTERS)

Stuck in ice, Walton's crew threaten to mutiny. Victor dies from exhaustion. Walton discovers the monster mourning the death of his creator. Walton calls him a hypocrite. The monster explains how he has been mistreated and misunderstood. He declares that justice has never been given to him and the only solution is to commit suicide now his creator has gone. He jumps from the cabin window and 'is lost in darkness and distance'.

? DID YOU KNOW?

A controversial view of *Frankenstein* was given by the critic Mario Praz: 'All Mrs Shelley did was to provide a passive reflection of some of the wild fantasies which, as it were, hung in the air about her'.

DETAILED SUMMARIES

CAPTAIN WALTON'S NARRATIVE (LETTERS 1–4)

LETTER 1 – 'A voyage of discovery to the land of knowledge'

❶ Captain R. Walton is writing to his sister, Margaret Saville.

❷ He describes his expedition to the North Pole.

Captain Walton is embarking on an ambitious expedition to the North Pole and is writing to reassure his sister Mrs Margaret Saville that his trip will be successful. He imagines that the Pole will be a beautiful region of 'light' (p. 13), is excited by the prospect that it is unknown and undiscovered, and hopes that he will be able to discover the secret of the magnet.

He reminisces on his early years which were spent passionately reading his uncle's collection of seafaring books. Against his father's dying wish, he spent six years training as a 'seafarer'.

We are introduced to the characteristics, values and desires of Robert Walton who is one of the main narrators (see **Structure**). His preoccupations reveal themes that are central to our understanding of the whole novel (see **Themes**). We see things from his perspective but we are also made to question his character.

Walton is a passionate, warm-hearted young man who is enthusiastic about his expedition. However, he might be led astray by the strength of his ambition and his longing for adventure. He has never been satisfied with what he has.

Walton's language is eloquent and fluent but this is deceptive because his ideas are confused. He contradicts himself when he says that the 'cold breeze' gives him a 'foretaste' of the Pole's 'icy climes' (p. 13) but then claims that he doubts that the Pole is 'the seat of frost and desolation' (p. 13). His strong imagination fantasises that 'snow and frost are banished' (p. 13) from the Pole. This is because the expedition was his 'favourite dream' (p. 14) as a child and explains why he *wants* to imagine the Pole as a beautiful place.

CHECKPOINT 1

What does Walton believe the North Pole will be like?

DID YOU KNOW?

The needle of a compass always points to the North Pole because of its magnetic attraction.

DID YOU KNOW?

The North Pole was discovered by Robert Peary only in 1909.

Walton – a modern Prometheus

Walton's desire to turn 'the favourite dream of his early years' (p. 14) into a reality can be seen as either heroic or simply self-destructive. His 'ardent curiosity' to see the Pole 'is sufficient to conquer all fear and danger or death' (p. 14). As a child, his imagination was carried away by his uncle's books on voyaging which later led him to experience 'cold, famine, thirst and want of sleep' as a sailor (p. 15).

Similarly, his motives for going are ambiguous. Walton says he wants to 'benefit' mankind by his discoveries (p. 14) but also admits that he prefers 'glory' to 'ease and luxury' (p. 15). In the legend, Prometheus steals fire from heaven to help mankind.

DID YOU KNOW?

'Prometheans' was the name given to the first safety matches, originally made in 1805 and later developed by Bryant and May.

LETTER 2 – Walton sets sail

1 He describes his success in finding a ship.

2 He states his need for a friend.

Three months have passed. Although Walton has found a ship and a crew, his 'enterprise' (p. 17) has been halted by bad weather.

Walton feels gloomy and lonely because he needs a friend who can support him when there are difficulties.

DID YOU KNOW?

Homer was an ancient Greek poet and creator of The *Odyssey*, which tells of an **epic** journey.

The importance of a friend

This seems a strange aspect of Walton's character. His need for a friend, however, is a theme of the novel. His letter-writing suggests that he needs someone with whom to share his experience but it is unlikely that he will actually meet anyone en voyage.

The need to have a friend is seen throughout the novel. Frankenstein travels with a valued friend, Frankenstein's monster tries to strike up friendships on several occasions. His need and the failure to have a female companion is the cause of his ultimate unhappiness.

He tells Margaret about two courageous members of his crew: the English lieutenant and the master.

Walton concludes that, even though he is despondent, he is still eager to start his exploration.

We are made to doubt Walton's vision in Letter 1 of the Pole as a region of 'eternal light' where 'the snow and frost are banished' (p. 13) because he has travelled further north to Archangel where he is surrounded by 'frost and snow' (p. 17). This **irony** makes us doubt Walton's vivid imagination. He is an unreliable **narrator**.

Walton admits that Coleridge's imaginative poem caused his love for the ocean (pp. 19–20).

The importance of friendship is stressed because Walton's deep desire for a companion is in conflict with his desire to explore. He admits that his complaints are 'useless' because he is unlikely to find a friend on 'the wide ocean' (p. 18).

DID YOU KNOW?

Coleridge published *The Rime of the Ancient Mariner* in 1798.

LETTER 3 – The voyage continues

❶ His ship is threatened by the ice.

❷ He resolves to continue with his voyage.

CHECKPOINT 2

What personal qualities does Walton value in his crew?

Three more months have gone by. It is now summer and Walton is nearer the Pole. Although he is safe, his vessel is threatened by the dangers of the 'stiff gales' and 'floating sheets of ice'. Despite this, Walton is optimistic, the crew are courageous, and they wish to go on. Walton assures Margaret that he will avoid putting his crew at risk unnecessarily.

We may justifiably question Walton's emotional stability. Optimistic in Letter 1, despondent in Letter 2, he is now again in 'good spirits'. It is unusual that the 'southern gales' give him a 'renovating warmth' (p. 21).

Walton's desire both to succeed in his voyage and reassure Margaret leads him to contradict himself. His promise that he 'will be cool' and 'prudent' is broken by his heated and ambitious **rhetorical questions** and exclamations at the end.

LETTER 4 – A friend at last

❶ Walton encounters two men on the ice.

❷ He brings one aboard – Victor Frankenstein.

❸ Frankenstein agrees to tell his life story.

A month later (5 August), Walton's ship is stuck in the surrounding ice. The crew is distracted by the astonishing sight of a 'gigantic' (p. 23) man on a sledge vanishing into the distance. The following morning they discover another traveller. Although he is approaching death, he is hesitant to come aboard. Walton revives him with brandy. However, he shows feverish interest in Walton's sighting of the other traveller.

Walton shares his ambitions with 'the stranger' (13 August) and his feelings for him grow into friendship. However, his friend is thrown into a wild despair when Walton confesses that he would sacrifice his own life in order to discover the knowledge which he desires.

Walton's curiosity is aroused (19 August) when the stranger wishes to tell him his life's history. He wants to warn Walton that an extreme desire for knowledge can be dangerous and hopes that Walton will be able to see a clear moral in the story he is about to tell. Walton resolves to record the story faithfully and send the manuscript to Margaret.

The importance of the setting

The remoteness of the setting prepares us for the strange sighting of the two travellers and the fantastic tale that Frankenstein intends to tell. The Pole's sublimity is suggested by the untamed wildness of the icy landscape.

Coleridge, a literary critic as well as a poet, talked of the importance of the 'willing suspension of disbelief', the way in which the reader is prepared to accept the impossible in order to enjoy a story.

In this novel, we are prepared to allow ourselves to imagine that in such a fantastic place fantastic things can really happen.

These letters set up a contrast between the two travellers. The creature is seen as 'gigantic', 'savage' and belonging to 'some undiscovered island' (p. 24). He is strange, different and unknown, whereas Frankenstein is an 'attractive' and 'amiable' (p. 26) 'European' who can speak English (p. 24). However, there is a tension between the light and dark aspects of Frankenstein's character: he has a 'double existence'. His emaciation and 'madness' can be lit up with 'a beam of benevolence' (p. 25).

CHECKPOINT 3

What is Walton's attitude towards Victor?

The attraction of knowledge emerges as the crucial theme of the whole novel. Frankenstein thinks Walton is like him because he is 'pursuing the same course' (p. 28). He sees it as his duty as a friend to warn Walton of the harm that knowledge can do; without friends, humans are only 'half made-up' (p. 27).

Now, take a break!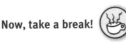

HH LEARNING CENTRE
HARROW COLLEGE

WHO SAYS ...?

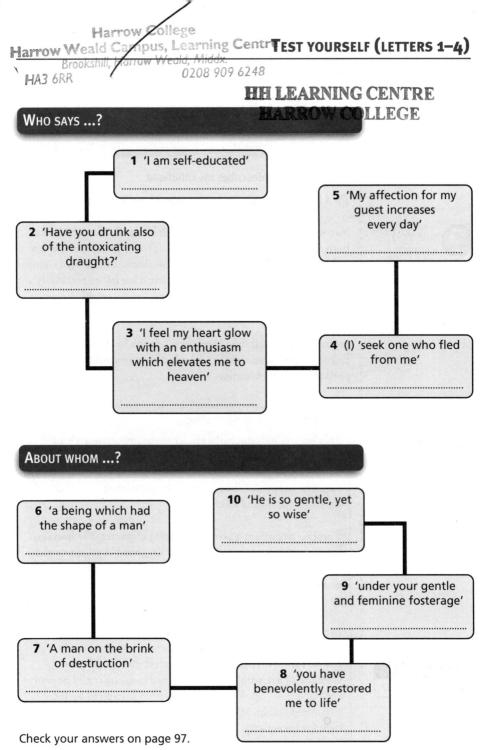

1 'I am self-educated'

....

2 'Have you drunk also of the intoxicating draught?'

....

3 'I feel my heart glow with an enthusiasm which elevates me to heaven'

....

5 'My affection for my guest increases every day'

....

4 (I) 'seek one who fled from me'

....

ABOUT WHOM ...?

6 'a being which had the shape of a man'

....

10 'He is so gentle, yet so wise'

....

9 'under your gentle and feminine fosterage'

....

7 'A man on the brink of destruction'

....

8 'you have benevolently restored me to life'

....

Check your answers on page 97.

Frankenstein **21**

VICTOR FRANKENSTEIN'S NARRATIVE (CHAPTERS 1–5)

CHAPTER 1 – Frankenstein's childhood

❶ Frankenstein describes his childhood.

❷ A key figure in his life is his foster-sister, Elizabeth.

DID YOU KNOW?

Percy, Mary Shelley's husband, was born into a wealthy family in Sussex, but was disinherited by his narrow-minded family.

Victor Frankenstein begins his tale with his family history. He was born into a wealthy Swiss family famous for its involvement in law and politics. His father, Alphonse Frankenstein, had married Caroline Beaufort. She had been left an orphan when her father, previously a rich merchant and Alphonse's best friend, lost his wealth, became a recluse and died. Victor was born on their travels in Italy.

He had a happy childhood and grew up with his foster-sister, Elizabeth. She was an orphan who had been rescued from a poor peasant family by Caroline.

The value of good parenting

This chapter introduces the reader to the importance Victor places upon the role of parents. He sees Caroline and Alphonse as responsible parents who 'fulfilled their duties' (p. 32) towards him. His happy childhood is entirely due to their 'stores of affection' (p. 33) and kindness.

Caroline emerges as a gentle and loving character. The heavenly language Victor uses to describe her suggests her goodness and virtue. She acts as a 'guardian angel' to Elizabeth. These qualities are echoed in Elizabeth who 'bears a celestial stamp in all her features' (p. 33).

Beaufort and Elizabeth's real parent, 'the Milanese nobleman' (p. 33), are seen as irresponsible fathers who unnecessarily plunge their own daughters into distress. Beaufort forces Caroline to live with him in a wretched isolation out of honour and 'false pride' (p. 30). Elizabeth's father is inspired by the 'antique glory' (p. 33) of Italy and leaves her behind in order to fight for his country.

CHECKPOINT 4

Who was Beaufort?

Victor Frankenstein is the main narrator of the novel. He tells Walton his version of events in the first person. Walton writes down what Victor tells him. His wish to reveal the cause of his misfortunes, which he had originally intended to keep secret, gives the story a personal and intimate feeling.

Victor is also the central character of his own story. His beliefs, passions and ways of judging other people and himself make a crucial contribution to the novel's meaning. This emphasises that *how* a story is told is as important as *what* is told.

Shelley uses minor characters here to help the reader judge the central characters. The two Romantic stories which relate the histories of Caroline and Elizabeth reveal a contrast between male and female attitudes.

CHAPTER 2 – Victor's early education

1 He describes his childhood in Geneva.

2 He develops his friendship with Henry Clerval.

3 He grows interested in books and science.

4 A lightning strike leads to his fascination with electricity.

This chapter shifts the focus to Victor himself who describes his character as a youth. Earlier we noted that Walton's fascination for the sea was inspired by 'Uncle Thomas's books' and *'The Ancient Mariner'* (pp. 17–19). We notice now that Victor's early imagination was similarly inspired by a book – by Cornelius Agrippa (p. 37) – and by what Agrippa wanted to achieve.

He explains that while from an early age Elizabeth loved nature and poetry, he yearned to discover explanations for the world around him. immortality, eternal youth, and the power to raise the dead. Victor feels that these events determine his destiny.

DID YOU KNOW?

The Philosopher's stone was, in the science of alchemy, the substance that has the power to transmute base metals into gold. It was also called 'the elixir'.

DID YOU KNOW?

Cornelius Agrippa was a German scholar (1486–1535) reputed to have raised people from the dead.

GLOSSARY

syndics chief magistrates

> ### The dangers of education
>
> The reader feels a sense of foreboding each time Victor reminds Walton that he has been ruined. He suggests that he has become the victim of his own passion. His 'thirst for knowledge' (p. 35) 'ruled (his) fate' which led to his 'destruction' (p. 40).
>
> The dangers of a strong imagination are signalled. His youthful 'bright visions' of success are contrasted with his later 'gloomy' condition (p. 37).

 DID YOU KNOW?

Luigi Galvani (1737–98) believed that electricity was to be found in the joints and muscles of animals.

Two years later, when a thunderbolt burns a tree to a stump, Victor feels that nature is so mysterious that science will never be able to explain the causes of things and he gives up his studies. However, his destiny to be a scientist cannot be avoided.

Note important differences between the characters of Elizabeth and Victor: she is calm, gentle and passive, whereas his 'violent' temper and 'eager desire to learn' (p. 36) would have made him 'sullen' without her influence. This characterisation prepares us for Victor's behaviour in Chapter 4 when he is away from Elizabeth.

Victor's admiration for his friend, Henry Clerval, reveals his own ambitious desire (p. 39). Clerval emerges as an imaginative and adventurous character who dreams of being famous. This extends the catalogue of dissatisfied male characters who are unable to let things be.

Note the mysterious attraction of science: nature's laws are 'secrets' that are 'hidden' (p. 36).

Chapter 3 – Victor at university

❶ Victor attends university.

❷ He is attracted by the teachings of two professors.

❸ He renounces his study of alchemy.

At seventeen, Victor's departure for the University of Ingolstadt is delayed by the death of his mother who, in looking after Elizabeth's fever, comes down with it herself. Victor's spirits rise when he considers what knowledge university would bring. On arrival at Ingolstadt, Victor meets two professors. He dislikes M. Krempe's brusque manner and the way he scorns his enthusiasm for alchemy. Victor, however, is not persuaded by Krempe's belief in the virtues of modern science. Despite this, he is overcome with inspiration by the other professor, M. Waldman, a chemist, who gives a rousing speech on the brilliance of modern science.

There is a conflict between Victor's studies and his relationships with others. He feels deep grief over his mother's death and sadness at having to leave his family to go to university. However, his gloomy loneliness is relieved by the prospect of acquiring knowledge.

Victor's obsession for study

This chapter begins a tension in Victor's priorities. His enthusiasm for study is developing into an obsession.

Victor is portrayed as an anti-social man who dislikes meeting strangers. He often judges people by their physical appearance. This is seen in his contempt for M. Krempe and his respect for M. Waldman. His studies are destructive to himself and his relationships with others.

DID YOU KNOW?

'Natural philosophy' was the term for 'science' when *Frankenstein* was written.

Waldman's declaration that only modern scientists have 'performed miracles' persuades Victor to abandon alchemy (p. 46).

CHECKPOINT 5

What is Waldman's opinion of Victor?

Notice the climax in Shelley's writing when she depicts Victor's emotional response to Waldman's lecture. His desire to 'explore unknown powers' creates inner 'turmoil' (p. 46).

CHAPTER 4 – Victor creates his monster

1 He becomes withdrawn from his family.

2 He becomes obsessed with the notion of creating a human being.

3 His health suffers as a result of his obsession.

CHECK THE BOOK

Before beginning *Frankenstein*, Mary Shelley and friends had been reading Coleridge's 'Christabel': 'Hideous, deformed and pale of hue', 'A sight to dream of, not to tell!'

Now obsessed with his scientific studies, Victor fails to visit his family for two years. He is possessed by an ambition to discover the cause of life and frantically digs up dead bodies from graveyards so that he can experiment upon them. Finally, he finds a way to give life to dead matter.

Astonished by his success, Victor goes a step further and stitches together a colossal man from the limbs of corpses whom he hopes to give life. Despite the beautiful spring and a worried letter from Alphonse, Victor is unable to tear himself away from his midnight labours.

The Gothic settings of the graves, churchyards, and dissecting-rooms evoke an eerie atmosphere.

DID YOU KNOW?

In Shelley's day, Prometheus was seen as a **symbol** of man's creative striving, and his revolt against the restraints of society.

There is a growing distinction between the inner world of the imagination and the outer world of reality. Victor is not repelled by his experiments because he feels that if he discovered a way to create life then mankind would 'bless' him for conquering death (p. 51). It is worth reminding ourself at this point that the novel has as its sub-title, *The Modern Prometheus*.

The effect on Victor of his obsession

His 'workshop of filthy creation' and his 'profane fingers' are details that suggest Victor now thinks his experiments are morally wrong (p. 52). Victor is at pains to show that he could not control himself. He appears possessed by an almighty force.

He fixes his sights upon 'one object of pursuit' (p. 49) which takes an 'irresistible hold' of him (p. 53).

Victor's isolation from society is clearly shown as a consequence of his obsession for scientific discovery. It emaciates him, makes him oblivious to daytime and the beauty of nature, and causes him to forget his friends and family.

CHAPTER 5 – The monster comes to life

1 **Finally the monster is born.**

2 **Victor is terrified by his creation.**

3 **He returns to his room with Clerval.**

On a 'dreary' (p. 35) night, Victor waits apprehensively for the body to come alive. The body shudders. The corpse breathes. Victor is filled with horror and rushes out of the room. He goes to bed, hoping to forget what he has done, but is disturbed by a nightmare about Elizabeth. He wakes but the monster is next to his bed, staring at him. Victor escapes again and passes the night and morning alone and tormented. Walking aimlessly, he bumps into his friend Clerval. Victor takes him back home and is wild with delight to find the monster has gone. His mad laughter and feverish behaviour frighten Clerval who has to look after him for five months.

Ironically, Victor fails to experience the sense of duty towards his creation that his own parents had felt for him.

Victor's dream hints at his underlying guilt. When he kisses Elizabeth she transforms into Caroline's corpse, symbolising that Victor's desires will bring destruction.

GLOSSARY

the Arabian Sinbad the Sailor

? DID YOU KNOW?

Dante was a thirteenth-century Italian poet who wrote *The Inferno* which describes the tortures of hell.

A turning-point in Victor's life

The changes in his behaviour are shown clearly

- He despairs at the ugliness of his creation
- He sees the consequences of his actions for the first time
- He abandons the creature twice
- He dreads its presence when it returns to his study

CHECKPOINT 6

Whose poem does Victor quote as he roams the street after creating his monster?

Clerval's appearance emphasises the importance that Shelley attaches to friendships. Victor feels a 'calm and serene joy' (p. 58) on seeing him, a feeling that contrasts with the enthusiastic frenzy of his experiments.

Now, take a break!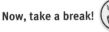

Who says ...?

1 'do not waste your time upon this; it is sad trash'

....

2 'The modern masters promise very little'

....

3 'A human being in perfection ought always to preserve a calm ...mind'

....

5 'Like one, that on a lonesome road/Doth walk'

....

4 'I shunned my fellow creature as if I had been guilty of a crime'

....

About whom ...?

6 'She was the living spirit of love to soften and attract'

....

7 'He loved enterprize, and even danger for its own sake'

....

10 'how very good you are to me'

....

9 'I did not remark before how very ill you appear'

....

8 'one hand was stretched out, seemingly to detain me'

....

Check your answers on page 97.

VICTOR'S NARRATIVE CONTINUES (CHAPTERS 6–10)

CHAPTER 6 – Victor's health recovers

❶ Victor finally returns to Geneva.

❷ He describes the changes in his family.

❸ His good spirits revive.

CHECKPOINT 7

Is Justine merely a servant in Elizabeth's house?

A letter from Elizabeth asks Victor to write home; Geneva is still the beautiful place it was in their childhood; little has changed. She explains that a servant girl, Justine Moritz, came back to their family after her mother died. Finally she describes the growth of Ernest, now sixteen, and William, Victor's younger brothers.

The importance of parenting

The stable, cheerful, and outdoor life of Victor's family contrasts with the change in Victor's health.

Elizabeth has replaced Caroline in the role of mother, implied by the way she refers to Victor's brothers as 'our dear children' (p. 62).

The relationship between Justine and her mother prefigures the relationship that will develop between the monster and Victor. Victor will feel guilty for his cruelty to the monster but will also blame him as the cause for his family's misery. Yet the monster is as much his creation as he is the creation of his parents!

Victor delays his return. Remaining at Ingolstadt, he introduces Clerval to his professors. He develops a dislike for science and turns to oriental languages. Time passes and Victor feels increasingly cheerful and back to his old self. Before he goes home, he takes a short tour of the countryside with Clerval.

Victor's decision to keep the monster an unspeakable secret causes an inner conflict, a tension that becomes more acute in the following chapters. His continual delays in returning home suggest a deep-rooted guilt.

Shelley uses irony to criticise Victor's behaviour. It is ironic that he is tormented by the praise Waldman and Krempe give him. It is also ironic that he realises his experiments were a 'selfish pursuit' (p. 67) but fails to acknowledge that his attempt to forget the creature by pursuing other interests is equally selfish.

CHAPTER 7 – Justine accused of murder

1 **Frankenstein's brother William is murdered.**

2 **Frankenstein quits Geneva.**

3 **He sees the monster in the mountains.**

4 **Justine is accused of the murder.**

On returning from his tour, Victor learns in a letter from his father that his youngest brother William has been strangled.

DID YOU KNOW?

Mary Shelley had a half-brother named William, who was five years her junior. She also had a little boy of her own, called William.

In despair, he leaves immediately for Geneva but arrives late. The city gates are shut. Taking a different route across the mountains, he is shocked to see the monster, who is suddenly lit up by lightning. The monster disappears. Victor immediately believes that the monster is the guilty murderer of William.

The monster's guilt

The uncanny appearance of the monster immediately after Victor's lament for William makes us associate the monster with dark and evil forces. Moreover, his appearance and William's death are so close as to suggest an inevitable connection.

There is conflict when Victor hears that Justine has been accused since he is convinced that the monster is the real culprit. The reader knows, however, that Victor's evidence would not stand up in court even though his description of the monster as a 'wretch' and a 'filthy daemon' (p. 71) make it plain that he is guilty of the murder.

At daybreak, Victor enters Geneva. He decides not to tell the authorities to chase the monster because they would probably not believe his story and think he was mad. When he arrives home, Ernest tells him that the murderer is their servant, Justine, but Victor is convinced of her innocence.

The cheerful tone at the end of Chapter 6 is quickly reversed by the news of William's murder. The theme of crime is introduced. The missing portrait of Caroline becomes an important piece of evidence in Chapters 8 and 16.

Shelley asks us to connect two incidents by the use of a motif. Victor covers his face with his hands when he reads the letter. This recalls his reaction (p. 59) when he imagines that the monster is in his apartment. Victor's inability to accept the monster may have disastrous consequences.

Shelley revels in describing images of **sublime** nature: thunder, lightning and the vast mountains create a tense, uncertain atmosphere.

CHECKPOINT 8

What is Alphonse's attitude towards Justine's court appearance?

? DID YOU KNOW?

Mary Shelley's stepmother's family came from Geneva, and she had been involved with a Genevese businessman before marrying William Godwin, Mary's father.

CHAPTER 8 – Justine is executed

1 Justine is put on trial.

2 She changes her plea to guilty and is executed.

3 Victor knows the monster is the culprit.

While Victor awaits Justine's trial, he blames himself for William's death. Although Justine appears calm and innocent, the case against her is strong. The public become suspicious. In her defence, she explains all the circumstances apart from one crucial piece of evidence: how she came to be wearing the portrait of Caroline. Elizabeth makes a speech defending Justine but it backfires.

CHECKPOINT 9

How does the court respond to Elizabeth's plea for Justine?

When, after a sleepless night, Victor returns to court he is astonished to find that Justine has confessed her guilt. Elizabeth and Victor visit her in prison, only to discover that the priest bullied her into confessing a lie. Justine is hanged.

A mockery of justice

Shelley introduces a crucial theme: the political theme of justice. She shows the unfairness of the legal system and reveals corruption in religious institutions. The 'mockery of justice' (p. 78) is seen by the way the judges prejudge Justine as guilty. It is a macabre **irony** that a man of God should cruelly abuse his power and force Justine to confess a lie. Notice how he makes her feel like a 'monster' (p. 83).

The crowd is portrayed as fickle. Their mean-minded prejudice is shown when they use Justine as a scapegoat for their anger.

The religious and legal language points out a contrast between the virtuous Justine and the immoral Victor: Justine, 'a saintly sufferer' becomes the second 'victim' to Victor's 'unhallowed arts' and 'lawless devices'. Victor confesses himself as the 'true murderer' (pp. 84-5).

CHAPTER 9 – Victor's remorse

1 **Victor is filled with misery about Justine.**

2 **He looks for comfort by journeying in the mountains.**

3 **He finds some sort of relief.**

Feeling responsible for the deaths of two innocent people, Victor wallows in solitude and gloom. His inner thoughts turn to revenge. Alphonse and Elizabeth are worried about him. The family retire to their other home at Belrive where Victor seeks relief from his feelings by journeying through the astounding scenery of the Alps.

The way Victor contradicts himself reveals his difficulty in coming to terms with the deaths of William and Justine. Victor confesses that he 'not in deed, but in effect, was the true murderer' (p. 89) but also wishes to revenge the 'crimes and malice' of the monster (p. 88).

Victor's desire to kill the monster gives Elizabeth's comment a dark irony: 'Men appear to me as monsters thirsting for each other's blood' (p. 88).

Shelley uses satanic language to underscore Victor's fall into despair. He wanders like an 'evil spirit' who feels a 'hell of intense tortures' (p. 86).

Now Victor's secret has affected the lives of others, he becomes even guiltier and more isolated. However, we feel that his 'deep, dark, deathlike solitude' will not solve any problems (p. 86).

DID YOU KNOW?

Robert Southey, a **Romantic** poet, called Byron and his friends the '**Satanic School**'.

CHAPTER 10 – Victor meets his monster

1 **Victor finally comes face to face with the monster.**

2 **The monster begs him to listen to his story.**

3 **They find shelter and the monster begins to tell his tale.**

Scaling a mountain of vast irregular beauty, Victor gazes at the desolate 'sea of ice'. In the mist, bounding towards him at frightening speed, is his creation. They speak to each other for the first time. Victor, accusing him of murder and wanting revenge for William's death, tries to kill him. The monster avoids his attack and pleads with Victor to listen to him. He explains how he has suffered because Victor abandoned him. He begs Victor for sympathy and implores him to listen to his tale. Victor agrees and they find shelter in a lonely hut. The monster begins his tale.

? DID YOU KNOW?
Of their visit to Switzerland, Percy Shelley wrote: 'I never imagined, what mountains were before.' They aroused in him: 'a sentiment of ecstatic wonder, not unallied to madness'.

The monster's surprising revelations

There are a number of surprises for the reader when we meet the monster. First, he does not seem to be a monster at all but a 'creature' p. 74 with very human and sensitive feelings. We feel sorry for his loneliness and admiration for his intelligence. The monster goes so far as to hint that he is guilty (p. 96) showing that he possesses a conscience.

Secondly, it is unexpected when the political concerns of Chapter 8 re-emerge in the monster's speeches. He demands 'justice', 'clemency', and 'affection' from Victor (p. 96).

His abandonment stresses Victor's responsibility towards him.

Finally, when the monster points out Victor's hypocrisy we are given an important new viewpoint of Victor's actions. The reader is made more critical of Victor's perception of things.

? DID YOU KNOW?
In the hotel register at Chamonix, Percy Shelley signed himself: 'P. B. Shelley, atheist, fool' – but in Greek!

We note Shelley's portrayal of nature as a grand, awesome and destructive power. The 'broken' and 'bent' trees, the 'jutting rocks', and the 'traces' of the 'avalanche' reflect the wreck that Victor has become mentally and physically (p. 93).

It is **ironic** that the monster chooses the moment to appear when Victor is feeling sorry for himself and about to 'forget the passing cares' (p. 93) of life. This illustrates Victor's self-deception.

CHECKPOINT 10

Why does Victor let the monster tell his story?

The monster's story is told in the barren, desolate and remote scene of the 'sea of ice' near the top of a mountain. This link to the setting behind Victor's tale, the North Pole, emphasises the isolation and doom of both these characters.

Now, take a break!

Who says ...?

1 'I had committed deeds of mischief beyond description horrible'

....

2 'I no longer see the world and its works as they before appeared to me'

....

3 'Everywhere I see bliss, from which I alone am irrevocably excluded'

....

5 'I confessed that I might obtain absolution'

....

4 'my soul glowed with love and humanity'

....

About whom ...?

6 'she accused herself for having caused the death of my brother'

....

7 'she fell into violent hysterics and kept her bed for several days'

....

10 'heroic and suffering'

....

9 'the first hapless victims to my unhallowed arts'

....

8 'The poor woman was very vacillating in her repentance'

....

Check your answers on page 97.

THE MONSTER'S NARRATIVE (CHAPTERS 11–16)

CHAPTER 11 – Early experiences

❶ The monster describes how he comes to Ingoldstadt.

❷ He finds a shelter by the De Laceys.

❸ He is attacked by the villagers.

The monster takes up the story, becoming the third main narrator Notice how the obscurity of the language in the opening illustrates the confusion of his first experiences. It is also significant that the monster is associated with night and we recall the circumstances of his creation (p. 56).

Victor tells Walton what the monster told him. The monster's character, attitudes and ways of judging people make a crucial contribution to the novel as a whole.

The monster's early life is crowded with confusion. He feels raw sensations but is unable to understand them or the world around him. He finds shelter in the forest and sleeps. He wakes in the night. Cold, frightened and alone, he cries. The first object he can make out is the moon and he is enchanted by it.

CHECK THE BOOK

J-J. Rousseau's *Emile* recommended that children should be brought up in natural surroundings away from the harmful influences of civilisation.

Sympathy for the monster

The enchantment he feels for the world around him reveals his true nature. His innocence is seen in the simplicity of his language and actions. His description of the birds as 'little winged animals' (p. 99) has a child-like quality. Although it is wrong for him to enter the old man's cottage and steal his food, he is unaware of this and means no harm.

His pleasure at hearing De Lacey's music, and his sorrow at the family's distress reveal him to be a creature of beautiful feelings and natural sympathies.

Our sympathies completely shift from Victor to the monster. Although Victor is a victim of the monster, the monster is clearly a victim of society and his own abandonment. His pain at being attacked by the villagers and his lack of understanding of the situation stress his vulnerability.

DID YOU KNOW?

Jean-Jacques Rousseau (1712–78) believed that man was born good but corrupted by society.

Gradually, the monster learns to distinguish between his senses. He starts to learn about the world by trial and error. He discovers the cause behind fire and tries to cook his food.

He enters a hut and an old man flees. He eats the man's dinner. Roaming across the fields, he reaches a village but the villagers brutally attack him. He flees and finds shelter in a hovel, attached to a cottage. He sees a young woman, a young man and an old man.

He observes their actions but does not understand what they mean.

CHAPTER 12 – The monster's education

1 **The monster watches the De Laceys at close quarters.**

2 **He tries to learn language.**

3 **He performs acts of kindness for the family.**

4 **He is horrified when he sees his own reflection.**

This chapter focuses on the monster's learning and his need to explain the world around him.

GLOSSARY

Pandaemonium chaos

DID YOU KNOW?

Percy Shelley was fascinated by science and while still at school at Eton was described as 'Engaged in nefarious scientific pursuits' including trying 'to raise the devil', by using electrical equipment.

The monster continues to watch the family in the cottage, trying to work out the reasons behind their behaviour. He is moved by the kindness that the young man and woman show towards the old blind man. He likes the family but is too frightened to join them. When he finds out that their sadness is caused by poverty, he collects firewood for them in the night.

The monster's natural kindness

The language creates an **ironic** parallel between the monster and Victor. We see scientific language in his wish to 'discover (the) causes' (p. 107) behind the De Lacey's unhappiness. Furthermore, his ambitions are emotionally charged for he 'ardently longed' and 'eagerly longed' (p. 109) to befriend the De Laceys. Unlike Victor, his attention and hopes are fixed on other human beings.

Friendly and virtuous actions come naturally to the monster. When he finds out that the De Laceys are poverty-stricken, he acts upon his knowledge by collecting firewood for them.

CHECKPOINT 11

What does the monster admire in the old man?

He discovers that they use language to communicate their thoughts and feelings. He passionately desires to learn language and starts to pick up the basics, hoping that one day he will be able to speak to the cottagers.

Admiring the beauty of the family, the monster is mortified when he sees his own reflection in a pool.

CHAPTER 13 – Parallels between the monster and Safie

❶ The family welcome Safie to their house.

❷ The monster learns about human society.

❸ He feels attracted to Safie.

In spring a beautiful woman arrives, an Arabian called Safie. Felix is overjoyed to see her and starts to teach her their language by reading from a history book called *Ruins of Empires*. The monster finds this an ideal opportunity to acquire language by listening from his hovel. Within two months he is able to understand everyday conversations. However, he learns things about mankind from *Ruins of Empires* which shock and disgust him. He is upset by the tales of war, injustice and abuse of power. Despite this, he is more pained when he learns about birth, children and families because this leads him to question his own origin, parentage and present isolation.

> **CHECKPOINT 12**
>
> What first impresses the monster about Safie?

The monster and Safie

The character of Safie is important because the De Laceys welcome her into their family, despite the difference of her appearance and culture. This contrasts with the rejection that the monster has experienced so far. He too has a different appearance yet he has been rejected.

This encourages him to believe that he can reveal hiself to the De Laceys and be accepted. This is all the more likely for old De Lacey is blind.

We see the emergence of the monster's sexual feelings. Although Agatha 'enticed' his 'love' (p. 103), he is separated by his ugliness. This contrasts with Felix who has a female companion in Safie.

This chapter is about the forces which shape the monster's personality. Like Victor, books are an important influence. Knowledge has a powerful effect on him. The more he learns about society, the less he seems to know about himself. He realises that he has no money, property, family, or friends. His question, 'What was I' (p. 117), shows a growing self-awareness of his own difference.

His natural goodness is shown by the way he turns away with 'disgust' at the deeds of 'bloodshed' described in *Ruins of Empires* (p. 115).

Chapter 14 – The De Laceys' troubled past

1 **The monster learns about the De Laceys' past.**

2 **He discovers why they welcome Safie.**

The monster is moved by the life story of the De Laceys. He discovers that they were a wealthy French family who had their wealth confiscated by the authorities because Felix had helped a Turkish merchant to escape from prison. He had been horrified when the French law had unfairly condemned the Turk to death. As a reward the Turk promised Felix his daughter, Safie's hand in marriage. They fell in love but Felix had to return to Paris because De Lacey and Agatha had been imprisoned for their involvement in the escape. They were all banished from France. Above this, Safie's father did not want to honour his promise to Felix. Safie, however, ran away from her father and found the De Laceys.

Like Victor, Felix's ambitions and reckless actions cause the plight of his family. (Chapters 7, 8, 21–23). However, Felix battles for justice and freedom whereas Victor imprisons the creature in isolation by his final refusal to complete his female mate (Chapter 20).

Persecution of the Turk by the French authorities reveals the corruption of the law. This injustice reflects Justine's mistreatment in Chapter 8.

CHECKPOINT 13

How does Safie reach safety?

A story within a story

At the centre of the book is another story. It is significant because it reveals more about the major characters and it develops the themes. However, the story links to events that will happen in the book as well as events that have already happened.

- The Turk's promise to reward Felix with his daughter, Safie and the subsequent breaking of the promise mirrors Victor's vacillation over creating a female mate for the monster (Chapters 17, 18 and 20).

- The Turk's 'tyrannical' (p. 122) mistreatment of Safie mirrors Victor's stubborn cruelty towards his child – the creature (Chapters 10 and 20).

- The Turk's ingratitude towards Felix is due to his religious differences. His prejudices reflect the misplaced hatred Victor and the whole of society have towards the creature.

CHAPTER 15 – The monster's education and suffering

❶ The monster acquires books.

❷ He discovers Victor's notes on his creation.

❸ He visits old Mr De Lacey.

❹ The rest of the family arrive and chase him out.

The monster learns to love virtue and hate vice from the story of the De Laceys. However, he experiences much more complex and advanced feelings when he reads three books which he found by chance. *The Sorrows of Young Werther* make him feel both joyous and sad. Plutarch's *Lives* helps him admire heroic leaders and despise tyrants. In contrast, *Paradise Lost* makes him identify his lonely state with Satan's banishment from heaven. Sometimes he becomes envious of the beautiful home of the De Laceys. When he discovers Victor's journal, which records how he was made, he is disgusted.

CHECK THE BOOK

Goethe's *The Sorrows of Young Werther* (1774), a novel told as a series of letters, describes an artist's love for a girl engaged to someone else. The artist eventually commits suicide.

CHECKPOINT 14

How does the monster learn of the circumstances of his creation?

One hope keeps him alive: the belief that the De Laceys will overlook his deformity and accept his friendship. He reveals himself to the blind old man when the others are out. When they return, the monster clings to De Lacey in fright. He is violently beaten by Felix, and flees in despair.

> ### The monster reveals himself
>
> The monster's decision to meet the blind old man alone inspires hope. The tone of calm sorrow of their conversation and the open-minded sympathy of De Lacey towards the friendless monster contrasts with the scene of brutal violence which follows. This shock emphasises the creature's reversal in fortune.
>
> Notice the importance of **viewpoint** (see **Themes**). Felix crucially misinterprets the creature's fearful clinging as an attack upon his father and forces the monster to run for his life.

CHECK THE BOOK

Satan's rebellion against God is the theme of John Milton's *Paradise Lost*, a very influential poem in Mary Shelley's day.

This chapter marks an abrupt change in the hopes, feelings and natural goodness of the monster. He portrays the agony of his desolation by comparing himself to Satan. Satan's rebellion against God is similar to the way the monster curses his creator upon finding the journal. The hellish isolation of his hovel compared to the 'bliss' (p. 125) of the cottagers' paradise makes him envious.

CHAPTER 16 – The monster as saviour and killer

❶ The monster resolves to find Victor.

❷ He saves a girl from drowning.

❸ Again he is attacked for his kindness.

❹ He describes the murder of William.

Finding his only bond to mankind broken, the monster is reduced to despair. He reflects that he revealed himself to De Lacey too hastily and he resolves to talk with him again. He is frightened when the family does not reappear. Felix returns and tells the landlord that they are leaving. Lonely and dejected, the monster releases his fury by burning the cottage.

> **The monster grows wicked**
>
> This chapter shows how the monster's exclusion by the De Laceys changes his character and destiny.
>
> The mood darkens with the deepening comparisons to Satan. The monster is portrayed as beast-like, powerful and destructive. Although he declares 'an everlasting war against the species' (p. 131) in revenge, he also seeks 'justice' from Victor (p. 134).

He decides to seek out his creator. On the way, he saves a young girl from drowning but a man shoots him.

CHECK THE FILM

Young Frankenstein (1974) directed by Mel Brooks is a devastatingly funny film with the monster as a tap dancer. It was photographed in black and white.

After two months, he arrives at Geneva and finds a young child whom he wishes to befriend. When the child reveals that he is William, a Frankenstein, the monster strangles him. He takes the miniature portrait of Victor's mother from the child's body. When he finds a barn to hide in, he sees a young girl sleeping. He is attracted to her but this makes him feel even more isolated and frustrated. In revenge, he places the portrait on her dress.

CHECKPOINT 15

What does the monster learn from saving the little girl?

Finally, he asks Frankenstein to create an ugly female companion for him.

The theme of prejudice is developed by the way William and the peasant misunderstand the monster's actions and intentions.

The monster's frustrated revenge will become tragic. The murdering of William and the framing of Justine make Victor mistrust him.

The sexual feelings the monster has towards Justine explain his demands for a female companion.

The monster's account finally unravels the mystery behind Caroline's portrait in Chapter 8.

Now, take a break!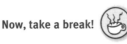

WHO SAYS ...?

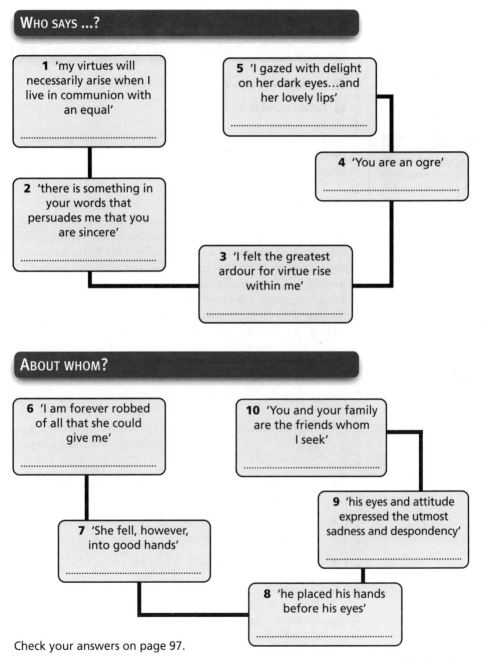

1 'my virtues will necessarily arise when I live in communion with an equal'

....

2 'there is something in your words that persuades me that you are sincere'

....

3 'I felt the greatest ardour for virtue rise within me'

....

4 'You are an ogre'

....

5 'I gazed with delight on her dark eyes...and her lovely lips'

....

ABOUT WHOM?

6 'I am forever robbed of all that she could give me'

....

7 'She fell, however, into good hands'

....

8 'he placed his hands before his eyes'

....

9 'his eyes and attitude expressed the utmost sadness and despondency'

....

10 'You and your family are the friends whom I seek'

....

Check your answers on page 97.

VICTOR'S SECOND NARRATIVE (CHAPTERS 17–24)

CHAPTER 17 – The monster's parting wish

❶ The monster wants Victor to make him a mate.

❷ Victor returns to his family home.

CHECKPOINT 16

Why precisely does the monster want a female mate?

Victor takes over the narrative for the second time. The form of spoken dialogue used in this chapter gives the reader a sense of immediacy and conflict.

The monster again asks Victor to create a female companion for him. Victor refuses, enraged by the monster's account of William's murder. The monster asks for sympathy and promises to live away from mankind, in peace, if Victor grants his wish. Victor is moved and changes his mind: he is persuaded that a female companion would stop the creature's misery and therefore remove the cause behind his crimes. The monster promises to reappear when Victor has created his mate. He leaves. In the dark Victor makes his way back to Chamonix but feels depressed by his promise.

A mate for the monster?

Victor is persuaded to make the female because:

- He fears the monster's power: 'I will revenge my injuries, if I cannot inspire love, I will cause fear.' (p. 141) Victor agrees 'to save' his family (p. 144).

- The monster is prepared to make sacrifices, promising to live with his mate 'cut off from the world' (p. 141).

- Victor feels guilty for abandoning the monster who explains that his crimes are due to a 'forced solitude' (p. 142).

- He is moved by the monster's pain and wishes to 'console him' (p. 142).

- He realises it is his moral duty. The creature demands the female 'as a right' (p. 140). Victor concludes it would be 'justice … to him and my fellow creatures' (p. 143) to comply.

He is aware that the monster began life as a naturally good being though Victor has doubts. If he makes another creature, then together they could cause even more destruction. They will not be able to keep themselves in exile, admiring the superior qualities of man. These concerns sow the seeds of Victor's inner conflict, self-doubt and misery.

Chapter 18 – Victor travels to England

1 **Victor decides he must go away to create a mate for the monster.**

2 **It is arranged that Clerval should travel with him.**

3 **Their journey takes them across Europe to London.**

Victor puts off his work, disgusted by the thought of creating another monster. Alphonse, however, thinks that Victor's gloom is because he is secretly in love with another woman.

Does Victor have another woman?

Victor's problems heighten and become more urgent when Alphonse proposes immediate marriage to Elizabeth. Victor's desire to please his aging father and the need to honour his mother's dying wish conflict with his plans to create the female. This causes tension and suspense.

The decision fuels Alphonse's suspicion that Victor loves another woman. This is a powerful dramatic irony since we know that he is 'bound' by 'indissoluble ties' to the creature (p. 95). He is indeed interested in another woman!

Alphonse questions him about his depression but Victor assures him that he loves Elizabeth. Alphonse is delighted and suggests immediate marriage. However, Victor puts it off, suggesting that a journey to England would solve his gloom. Secretly, Alphonse arranges for Clerval to join Victor on his trip. This thwarts Victor's plans to create a new monster in secrecy. As they travel through Europe, Clerval enjoys the beautiful scenery but Victor cannot stop thinking about his promise to the monster.

CHECK THE BOOK
William Wordsworth's 'Tintern Abbey' is one of the most famous poems in English **Romantic** literature. No wonder Shelley uses a quotation from it in this chapter to describe Clerval's love of nature.

This chapter deepens Victor's inner conflicts. Although he feels a duty towards the monster he also feels guilty for endangering humanity.

Caught between these divided responsibilities, he deceives himself by delaying his work and avoiding his family. Notice how this conflict increases his isolation.

Clerval is used to present Victor with an image of his 'former self' (p. 153). Clerval's joy and 'enthusiastic imagination' (p. 151) only deepen Victor's gloom and serve to remind us of the contrast between the destinies of these two characters.

CHAPTER 19 – Victor starts his new creation

❶ Victor and Clerval journey to Scotland.

❷ Victor settles in an isolated hut.

❸ He commences his work.

This chapter focuses on Victor's difficulty in dealing with the tension between his travels with Clerval and his need to create the female creature.

CHECKPOINT 17

Why does Alphonse arrange for Clerval to go with Victor on his travels?

Victor finds himself lured into peace and happiness by Clerval. He feels presumptuous because the creature has no friends and because he knows that making a second creature will cause him misery.

In October, Victor and Clerval arrive in London and stay there until March. Victor, feeling guilty about the past and fearing the future, avoids company as much as possible. Eventually, they take a journey to Edinburgh and stop off at various places on the way. Victor leaves Clerval and goes to the remote Orkney islands; he is worried that he has delayed his task for so long that the monster might harm his family. He hires a shabby hut where he starts creating the new monster. This time, he is sickened and horrified by his work.

 DID YOU KNOW?

Cumberland in the Lake District was the home of the **Romantic** poets, William Wordsworth and Samuel Taylor Coleridge.

Victor deceives himself in a more surprising way. His claim that he was 'guiltless' (p. 157) is an astounding contradiction of all the facts.

Shelley develops an atmosphere of claustrophobia; Victor, who is 'embittered … by the memory of the past and the anticipation of the future' (p. 155), is clearly haunted by the monster from all angles.

CHAPTER 20 – A change of plans and location

1 Victor talks to the monster.

2 He decides against completing the creation of a mate.

3 He sails out and disposes of his unfinished creation.

4 He drifts ashore on the Irish coast.

This chapter signals a dramatic turning point in the destinies of Victor and the monster.

The opening reveals Victor absorbed in his own thoughts. His inability to escape from his own doubts creates a mood of private claustrophobia.

One dark evening Victor has doubts. He concludes it will be wrong to create another monster. When he looks up, he sees the creature at the window, grinning, and suddenly he destroys the half-finished monster. The howling and anguished monster threatens Victor but he remains firm in his decision not to create a female companion. The creature leaves with the haunting words, 'I shall be with you on your wedding night' (p. 163).

Victor sails out in a little boat and drops the remains of the creature into the sea. He falls asleep in the boat. When he wakes, he finds that the high wind has taken him far into the ocean. Eventually, he sees land and arrives on the shore of Ireland. Strangers surround him on the beach, accuse him of murder, and take him to court.

When Victor arrives in Ireland, parallels between Victor and the monster are strengthened. Victor, now a foreigner, is not welcomed by the prejudiced and suspicious crowd. He now feels what it is to be like an innocent victim.

CHECK THE FILM

Boris Karloff played the monster in *Frankenstein* (1931).

CHECKPOINT 18

How does Victor come to land in Ireland?

GLOSSARY

Superscription the name and address at the head of a letter

Is Victor right to destroy the female?

When the female is destroyed, the reader's sympathies are divided between Victor and the monster. We view this incident from both their perspectives.

His monster does appear to have some basically good qualities and his assurance that he wants nothing more than a female mate seems quite convincing. We have noted throughout the novel that he is attracted to women so asking for a mate of his own is a natural enough request.

In a way, Victor's destruction of the female is symbolic. Most female characters in the book are life-givers whereas the male characters appear ambitious and destructive.

CHAPTER 21 – Another murder trial

❶ Victor is put on trial for the murder of Clerval.

❷ He falls ill and spends months in prison.

❸ He is found innocent and travels home.

CHECKPOINT 19

How had the murdered man died?

Forming a clear parallel to Chapter 8, Victor now replaces Justine as the victim on trial. Witnesses come forward to give their evidence against him. He remains calm when the first man relates how he found a dead body on the beach until he mentions that there were black fingermarks on the neck. Realising that his monster has done the deed, Victor almost faints but this arouses the suspicion of the magistrate, who asks Victor to see the corpse, wanting to observe his reaction. When Clerval's body is revealed, Victor's shock arouses more suspicion.

Victor falls ill and spends two months in a prison cell. His fever is so strong he is barely conscious of his surroundings. He recovers and the magistrate tells him that evidence has been found which proves his innocence. Victor is relieved from his despair by his father.

Parallels in the novel

Like Justine Victor is wrongly tried for murder. This trial, however, ends with the correct verdict but not before Victor has spent two unpleasant months in prison.

The moral themes of crime, justice, and freedom are developed as the prison takes on a symbolic role (see **Themes**). Victor's imprisonment mirrors the monster's lack of freedom in his hovel. The mental barrier that Victor felt between himself and society (p. 153) now becomes a shocking reality.

He knows the sense of isolation that the monster feels. The only comfort he has is in the companionship of his friend Henry Clerval. It is friendship which Walton desperately needs on his expedition to the North Pole. And friendship which the monster wants from a female mate.

CHECK THE BOOK

Mary's father's book, *An Enquiry Concerning Political Justice* (1793) had greatly impressed the English **Romantics**.

Shelley contrasts this incident with the birth of the creature by repeating the motif of the 'hand' 'stretched out' (p. 174). Unlike Alphonse, Victor ran away from his son. Now his father arrives, claims his son and takes him home.

GLOSSARY

maladie du pays homesickness

laudanum a medicine that includes opium

sophisms eloquent but deceptive arguments

CHAPTER 22 – Victor and Elizabeth are married

1 Victor travels to Paris.

2 A letter from Elizabeth hastens his return to Geneva.

3 They are married.

Victor has a rest from the journey in Paris. Alphonse is worried by Victor's habit of shutting himself away from company and blaming himself for the deaths of Justine and William.

In May, Victor receives a letter from Elizabeth. She declares her love for him but is anxious to know whether he is in love with another woman. The letter reminds him of the monster's threat, 'I shall be with you on your wedding night' (p. 163), but he writes back expressing his love for her and his wish to be married. However, he warns her that he has a secret which he will tell her after the wedding.

Elizabeth's letter speeds up the marriage subplot and, in turn, the oncoming conflict promised by the monster.

When Victor and Alphonse arrive in Geneva, preparations are made, and Elizabeth is married to Victor. They decide to go to Italy by boat for their honeymoon. They enjoy the beautiful scenery and stop in Evian for the night. The sun is gradually sinking.

Victor's tragic blindness reaches new heights and fills the reader with a sense of oncoming catastrophe.

Victor's guilt is misplaced. He is disturbed by the fact that he created the monster when he should see that his failure to act as a parent to the monster has caused the deaths of William, Justine and Clerval.

Victor's misinterpretation of the monster's words, 'I shall be with you on your wedding night' reveals Victor's deepening self-absorption. His belief that the monster will kill him, rather than Elizabeth, has a peculiar **dramatic irony**.

? DID YOU KNOW?

Evian, famous for its mineral water, was a fashionable spa resort on the southern shores of Lake Geneva.

CHAPTER 23 – Murder and death

❶ Victor paces the house to ensure that his bride is safe.

❷ She is murdered by the monster in his absence.

❸ Victor's father dies.

❹ He swears to destroy his creation.

It is their wedding night. The moon appears and the wind rises. Terrified in the darkness and awaiting his own death, Victor spends an hour looking around the house for the monster. He is happy that it is nowhere to be seen. Suddenly he hears Elizabeth scream from the bedroom. He finds her dead with black fingermarks on her neck. He sees the monster grinning at the window and shoots at him. Victor assembles a party of people from the inn and they pursue the monster but fail to find him.

CHECK THE FILM

The Bride of Frankenstein is one of nearly sixty films which use the Frankenstein story.

Frankenstein's bride

This is the central episode on which so many horror films are based, when the bride is murdered in the bridal suite by the monster. Shelley creates tension in the reader by the dark atmosphere of the storm and the blind nervousness of Victor.

Part of the horror derives from the fact that Victor is away from his bride checking the inn for safety when she is murdered. He is alerted by the terrifying scream, the stuff of nightmares.

The destruction of Elizabeth is a clear parallel to Victor's destruction of the monster's female companion. Now, however, the tables are turned.

Victor returns to Geneva with the miserable news. The misfortune is too much for Alphonse, who dies.

Victor's last resort is to tell a magistrate the whole story of the creation and the monster's foul deeds, hoping that the law will hunt him down. The magistrate promises the monster will be suitably punished should he ever be found.

CHECKPOINT 20

Why does the magistrate try to arrest the monster?

The death of Alphonse strengthens the likeness between Victor and the monster: they both lack family and friends. They also become linked by their mutual revenge, when Victor decides to pursue the monster (**see Themes**).

The judge's disbelief of Victor's story blasts his final hope of justice and he vows to devote himself to the destruction of his monstrous creation.

CHAPTER 24 – The pursuit of the monster

❶ Victor begins his pursuit of the monster.

❷ He follows the tracks across Europe and Russia.

❸ The chase leads him to the north.

❹ He is saved by Walton.

DID YOU KNOW?

The **Romantic** writers were very enthusiastic readers of early travel books and were inspired by them.

Victor, furious for revenge, resolves to kill the monster or die in the attempt and is prepared to chase him across the world. Before he leaves Geneva, he goes to the graveyard and calls on the spirits of the dead to help him in his revenge. He hears the monster's laugh bellow in his ears.

Victor pursues the monster for months over land and sea. When Victor loses his tracks the monster taunts him by leaving signs and messages. This only serves to deepen Victor's passion to kill him.

Travelling towards the North Pole, Victor hires a sledge and dogs to chase his enemy. He almost catches him but they are separated when the ice splits apart. Victor find himself sinking when he sees Walton's ship.

Victor ends his narrative by pleading with Walton to kill the monster if he ever sees him. Victor's request that Walton should destroy the creature is crucial to setting up the final climax of the novel.

> **The setting for the chase**
>
> The scope of the setting becomes global as Victor hunts down the monster. The quest becomes an epic one, to put it in Victor's words, 'And now my wanderings began which are to cease but with life.' (p. 195)
>
> The trail takes him from the 'blue Mediterranean' to the 'wilds of Tartary and Russia' (pp. 196–7). Finally, he turns northwards and retraces the route taken by his saviour, Walton, and we rejoin the story where we started with the first letter to Mrs Saville.

There is a confusion of roles: it is difficult to decide which character has the upper hand and who is pursuing whom. Victor pursues the monster in a sledge but the monster taunts Victor in the graveyard and leaves him food to keep him alive.

The monster's actions clearly suggest that he wants Victor to experience, and suffer, the same fate as himself. The two characters seem to merge: they are both isolated, hate each other, but are also fatally linked.

CHECK THE FILM
Frankenstein Meets the Wolf Man (1943) suggests an episode which Shelley must have omitted!

Notice that Shelley reveals how revenge is self-destructive: 'I was cursed by some devil and carried about with me my eternal hell' (p. 197).

Victor's sighting of the ship brings us back to the start of the book from a new perspective.

Now, take a break!

WHO SAYS ...?

1 'I felt that I had no right to share their intercourse'

....

2 'I fancy it will go hard with you'

....

3 'Do you not love another?'

....

4 'You have determined to live, and I am satisfied'

....

5 'I will preserve my life; to execute this dear revenge...'

....

ABOUT WHOM ...?

6 'Man ... how ignorant art thou in thy pride of wisdom'

....

7 'His soul overflowed with ardent affections'

....

8 'He rose and quitted the room with my nurse'

....

9 'What agonizing fondness did I feel for them'

....

10 'the best hope and the purest creature'

....

Check your answers on page 98.

WALTON'S SECOND NARRATIVE (THE FINAL LETTERS)

DEATHS

1 Walton's vessel is ice-bound.

2 Victor dies.

3 The monster makes his final appearance.

The narrative comes back full circle as Robert Walton provides us with the final and unexpected climax to the novel.

DID YOU KNOW?

Mary Shelley's mother had originally been involved with a, Captain Gilbert Imlay, an American, who had made many expeditions into the wilder parts of America.

26 August 'Lost in the darkness and distance'

Walton resumes as the narrator. He portrays Victor as a tragic figure: a great man who has become a wreck and who knows the 'greatness of his fall' (p. 203).

Victor is a **Romantic** hero. Despite his moral tale on the dangers of knowledge and ambition he still feels the need to be 'engaged in any high undertaking' (p. 205).

He tells Margaret that Victor told this strange story with great passion but admits that he would not have believed it to be true unless Victor had shown him the letters between Felix and Safie. He laments that Victor must have been a great man before his misfortunes and is worried that Victor's health is declining.

2 September

Walton's ship is surrounded by huge glaciers. Faced with the prospect of sinking, he realises that he has endangered the lives of his crew and his 'mad schemes are the cause' (p. 205). Although they are stuck, Victor rouses the hopes of the sailors.

5 September

Still surrounded, Walton's crew threaten to mutiny unless he decides to abandon his expedition once the ice moves.

Walton's reaction to his crew's threats mirrors Victor's initial response to the creature: Walton cannot 'in justice ... refuse this demand' (p. 206). Victor, however, gives a rousing speech, urging them to continue their great enterprise. He tells them it is shameful to abandon a glorious pursuit at the first sight of danger. The crew appears moved by his opinion It is ironic that Victor seems ignorant of the moral of his own tale when he makes his elevated speech, urging on the crew.

7 September

The ironies deepen when Walton, who is responsible for the fate of his crew, feels that he has been made a victim of their unfair demands. Eventually, he gives way to the crew's wishes and agrees to return to England if the ice clears.

12 September

The ice has cleared and Walton is returning to England disappointed that his friend, Victor Frankenstein, has died. Victor believed, in his last moments, that he was not blameworthy for the monster's actions but urged Walton to avoid ambition. While Walton is writing the account of his death he hears a strange noise from Victor's cabin.

In Victor's cabin he meets the monster who seems both gleeful at the death of Victor and upset. Walton accuses him of hypocrisy. The monster replies that he cannot believe how he has been a murderer

 CHECK THE FILM

Frankenstein Unbound (1990) Based on Brian W. Aldiss's novel, and directed by Roger Corman, John Hurt plays a time-traveller who goes back to the summer when Mary wrote her novel.

because he started his life with the intention of doing good and experiencing life in the company of mankind. He reminds Walton that mankind has only given him hate for his good actions and that he has been a sufferer of the worst injustices. He is so disgusted by his deeds of revenge that there is now only one course of action: he must kill himself. The monster then climbs out of the window and disappears into the darkness.

Closing thoughts

Victor's last words show his inability to accept his moral message to 'avoid ambition' for he realises that 'another may succeed' in 'science and discoveries' (p. 210).

Walton's despondency at losing his friend and his desire to carry out Victor's dying wish to destroy the monster explain his reproaches to the creature.

The monster's final Romantic speech sums up the tragedy and the issues of the book. It shows the contrast between his early goodness and his evil revenge. It explains clearly that his rejection by his creator and the rest of humanity was an 'injustice' (p. 213).

The reader is finally left uncertain whether the monster fulfils his promise to burn himself, for he is 'lost in darkness and distance' (p. 215).

Now, take a break!

Test yourself (the final letters)

Who says ...?

1 'Am I thought to be the only criminal ,when all humankind has sinned against me?'

....

2 'Did you not call this a glorious expedition?'

....

3 'If we are lost, my mad schemes are the cause'

....

5 'Evil thenceforth became my good'

....

4 '(my purpose) is assigned to me by heaven'

....

About whom ...?

6 'like a volcano bursting forth, his face would suddenly change to an expression of the wildest rage'

....

7 'he was sunk in languor and almost deprived of life'

....

8 'And do you dream?'

....

10 'He is dead who called me into being'

....

9 'you have a husband and lovely children'

....

Check your answers on page 98.

PART THREE

COMMENTARY

THEMES

THE MEANING OF THE MONSTER

At the heart of *Frankenstein* are a number of questions: the monster asks 'Who was I?' and 'What was I?' The answers still remain an enticing mystery. Many readers have put forward different views.

Frankenstein can be read on many levels. The novel has been seen as:

- A moral tale: a parable about the conflict between good and evil, or a warning about the dangers of scientific progress.

- A **Romantic** tale: the novel explores the tragic ruin of two heroes. Victor and the monster become powerful **symbols** of loneliness who are destroyed by their own talents and needs.

- A psychological tale: the monster stands for the destructive quality of 'unnatural' desires and dangerous ambitions, or the dark side of Victor's personality on the rampage.

- A social tale: it is about a parent/child relationship showing the sad consequences of a father failing to perform his duties.

- A political tale: the monster symbolises people who have been denied their natural rights of freedom, equality and fraternity. Victor stands for a tyrannical ruler.

- A philosophical tale: which asks 'What is the origin of evil?' Does it arise from our nature or does it come from the world around us – from society? The creature begins as a good character but becomes a monster by the cruel and monstrous ways humans treat him (see **Setting and background**).

The best way for you to develop your own interpretation is to study the themes of the book and how they are developed by looking at:

- Events and how they are portrayed

- Characters, their views, and how they are portrayed

- Key images which are repeated in the language

The main themes are: knowledge, ambition, prejudice, justice.

 DID YOU KNOW?
When Mary Shelley was writing her book at Byron's villa, a fellow-guest, Dr Polidori, was also writing his horror story, *The Vampyre*, which was mistakenly published under Lord Byron's name in 1819.

KNOWLEDGE

Discovery

Walton, Victor and the monster all begin their stories by expressing a deep desire to explain the world around them, which is like an unknown mystery waiting to be discovered (**see Language**). Each has a different focus. The monster wants to 'discover the motives' behind the De Laceys' behaviour and to 'unravel the mystery' (p. 107) of language. His humble aims are human, social, and arise from necessity. Victor and Walton, however, have lofty ambitions and are prepared to sacrifice human relationships in order to fulfil them. Victor's 'eager desire' to find the 'secrets of nature' (p. 38) and Walton's 'ardent' passion to explore 'a part of the world never before visited' (p. 14) of the North Pole take them away from their loved ones and into isolation. However, their sacrifices are much deeper and more disturbing than this.

AMBITION

The central concern of the book is the moral consequences of ambition. Walton and Victor may have good intentions to be 'benefactors' to mankind by discovering great things, but as a result Victor destroys himself and those around him, and Walton puts his crew at risk. They fall victims to their uncontrollable passion to realise their dreams. Both characters are only partially aware of their surroundings and what they are doing. Victor is only able to see with hindsight that his experiments on corpses are immoral and 'unhallowed acts' (p. 179) and Walton's fantasy that 'snow and frost are banished' (p. 13) from the North Pole is shown in stark contrast to the real facts.

Real problems occur when the ambitions of Victor and Walton endanger the lives of other people. Unlike Victor, Walton abandons his 'mad schemes'. He saves his crew, but reluctantly. Victor, however, is so wrapped up in the process of making his creature, that he fails even to consider what his responsibilities towards it will be once it comes alive. Victor's ambitions are selfish and quite the opposite of a benefit to mankind!

 DID YOU KNOW?

At the time Mary Shelley was writing, the Industrial Revolution was in full swing, and many new inventions were being made.

? DID YOU KNOW?
In Greek myth, Prometheus's punishment was to be chained to a cliff, where an eagle pecked daily at his liver!

PREJUDICE

There are many examples in the book of characters who are prejudged, misunderstood and victimised by others, which leads to their rejection, isolation and despair.

Social corruption

Justine, the Turkish Merchant and Victor are oppressed by people who crassly abuse their authority. Justine is wrongly put to death by judges who 'had rather ten innocent should suffer than that one guilty should escape' (p. 82). She is also forced to confess a lie by a priest. Similarly, the Turk is condemned to death because the French authorities dislike his race, values and culture, which are different from their own.

? DID YOU KNOW?
When *Frankenstein* was written, it was still legal to buy and sell slaves.

Fear of difference

People's fear of things which are unknown to them, or which they do not understand, can bring out the worst in them – namely, mental cruelty and physical violence. People oppress other people by attacking, excluding, or imprisoning them, in order to control the source of this fear. Victor is treated roughly and brought in front of a magistrate by the suspicious Irish crowd because he is foreign. Justine is tormented by the crowd because they have already labelled her a child-murderer. Most obviously, the monster is beaten by the villagers because of his ugly physical appearance. They do not judge him by his actions or seek to understand him.

DID YOU KNOW?

In a number of European countries, you are 'guilty' unless you can prove your innocence. In British law, you are considered innocent until you are proved guilty.

Imprisonment

The prison is an important **symbol**. The imprisonment of Justine and Victor are injustices because they are both innocent. The monster has to retreat into a hovel, a symbol of his social exclusion, rejection and isolation. It is his prison.

Viewpoint

People's inability to see the true reality beneath the appearance of things is a central theme. The window or frame is a symbol of how we view things. Many characters are mentally imprisoned by their own perspectives. Until Chapter 11, we see the monster as a 'devil' (p. 95) because this is how Victor sees him. We get a big shock when the monster speaks. His thoughts are beautiful. When Victor sees him at the window of his hut in the Orkneys he describes him as full of 'treachery' (p. 161). We do not believe him. It is only now we see that Victor's prejudices have clouded his judgement. There are two perspectives of the creature: a 'feeling and kind friend' or a 'detestable monster' (p. 129). William, the nurse, Felix, the old man, the peasant, Mr Kirwin and the Turk all have limited viewpoints.

The monster in man

There are many instances when we feel that the humans are more monstrous than the monster. Shelley could be using the monster as a symbol for our own inner ugliness or the animal side of man's nature. Although the monster appears to be the cause of fear and prejudice, he might stand for our ugly and violent reaction to something unknown and different.

DID YOU KNOW?

Other **Gothic novels** use this idea, like R. L. Stevenson's *Dr Jekyll and Mr Hyde*.

JUSTICE

The source of conflict between Victor and the monster is explored thoroughly in their arguments in Chapters 10 and 17. The monster knows that he has been the victim of foul injustices at the hands of humans and he wants Victor to correct these wrongs.

Parental duties

The monster sees himself as the son of Victor when he says: 'I am thy creature: I ought to be thy Adam, but I am rather the fallen angel' (p. 96), and demands that Victor fulfil his 'duty' as a father.

His deeds of revenge and mischief are due to pain, suffering and abandonment; this makes Victor partially responsible for the deaths of William and Justine. Victor cannot give the monster friendship because he cannot forgive him for William's murder. However, Victor does realise that he has 'no right' to withhold the gift of a female creature and that it would be 'justice' to create her (pp. 142–3). To deny him a mate is to deny him of his natural right to fraternity.

Companionship

The need for love, whether from friends, family or a partner, is a crucial issue in the novel. Victor's early years are portrayed as a paradise. Unlike the monster, he has no longing for love and affection because his parents 'were possessed by the very spirit of kindness and indulgence' (p. 36). Close relationships are depicted as a life-giving force. There are many instances of one character being 'restored to life' by the kind acts of another. Walton and Clerval both restore Victor to life and Safie restores the 'spirits' of Félix. Nature is also seen as a friend with the power to lift a human out of gloom and anxiety. Victor brings the creature back to life but fails to act as his friend.

Denial and guilt

Like Justine's mother, Victor is 'very vacillating' (p. 64) in his repentance. He is caught in a vicious cycle between his duty to the monster and his duty to friends, family and mankind at large. He has no hard evidence of the monster's good deeds, only evidence of bad ones. He begins to distrust the monster and starts to have doubts about his promise. He first thinks that he would be saving mankind from the monster's revenge if he makes the creature a mate, but changes his mind when he considers that the monster might be just tricking him. His destruction of the female mate is tragic and is a consequence of Victor's growing paranoia and self-absorption, which in turn is a consequence of his guilt. Victor's feeling that he has 'unchained an enemy' (p. 179) among his family and friends makes him avoid them. Victor's inability to face up to his actions and tell his secret to someone ruins his relationships before the monster causes devastation.

CHECK THE FILM
Frankenstein Created Woman (1966) has Victor giving life to a woman with the soul of her dead lover. Strangely enough, a murder spree ensues!

Revenge and destruction

Victor's refusal to make the female is a denial of the creature's human rights. Victor does not treat him as a human so he does not act like one. He truly lives up to his name as a 'monster' and ceases to be a 'creature'. The climax of the novel is taken up with the theme of revenge. It is only by revenge and punishment that the monster can feel that some justice has been done. He evens up the score by subjecting Victor to the same despair that he has experienced all his life. He kills his friend. He sets Victor up as the suspect. Victor experiences prejudice. Victor endures imprisonment. Finally, the monster **symbolically** destroys Victor's female companion, Elizabeth. The novel ends with them in mutual pursuit and combat. These two characters become exactly like each other. We do not know who is the monster and who is the 'victor'. We know from Shelley's diaries that she felt revenge is a savage and destructive emotion and this is made clear in the monster's final speech. He declares tragically that he finds his crimes and his character abhorrent. The only solution is suicide.

CHECK THE NET

Look up Henry Fuseli's painting *The Nightmare* and compare it to the description of Elizabeth's death.

STRUCTURE

The author shapes a novel to ensure that the purposes of the work are communicated effectively to the reader. He or she will choose to position events and ideas in a particular order and will decide to present them through particular forms.

Handling of time

The events in *Frankenstein* do not happen in chronological order. The novel begins after most of the action has already happened. To understand the mystery behind Walton's sighting of the creature and the decayed condition of Victor, the author returns to the past by using **flashbacks**. We go back to Victor's childhood and life at university but then William's murder creates a new mystery. In order to understand the lead-up to this event, Shelley turns the clock back to the early years of the monster. The two stories then converge. The final section of the novel explores the relationship between the creature and Victor. This brings us back full circle to the opening but we see Walton's ship from Victor's perspective this time. The very last section is the real dramatic climax to the novel where the three main male characters are brought together.

DID YOU KNOW?

When Mary Shelley wrote *Frankenstein*, very few novels had ever been written.

One effect of this technique is to show the influence the past has on the present. It emphasises how the fate of Victor and the monster are inseparable. This links to the theme of guilt: both the monster and Victor are haunted by their past actions, which keep returning in their minds and crush their spirits.

Narrators

Victor is the main narrator who tells Walton what the monster told him. Walton writes down for his sister what Victor told him. Each story is enfolded within another story: this is called **chinese-box narration**. This helps the reader feel that we are going deeper into the story; it shows that behind every story there is another story told from a different point of view.

? DID YOU KNOW?
Many early novels were epistolary – that is, written in the form of letters.

LETTERS 1-4
by Captain Robert Walton

CHAPTERS 1-10
Victor Frankenstein's narrative

CHAPTERS 11-16
The Monster's tale

CHAPTERS 17-24
Victor Frankenstein's narrative

CHAPTER 24-THE END
Letters by Captain Robert Walton
including a continuation of **The Monster's tale**

Shelley uses three narrators who tell their stories through their own eyes. We see the tale through different perspectives or angles. These viewpoints are all limited and biased, which helps us to make up our own minds about the characters and explore the novel with freedom. However, this technique does have a clear effect on our feelings: we feel sympathy for Victor in the first section, change our sympathies when we meet the monster, and experience divided sympathies in the final section.

Authentication

The letters of Walton and his manuscript of the story make the extraordinary events appear more believable for us. Victor's evidence of the letters between Felix and Safie, in turn, make Victor's story about the monster seem more credible for Walton. Walton's meeting with the monster at the end of the tale finally vindicates Victor's tale. The story cannot be reduced to a delirious fantasy of his deranged mind although Victor's wild style might have an edge of madness (see **Language and style**).

Contrasts and parallels

Shelley structures her story by using contrasts and parallels. She loves repeating her ideas with slightly different variations. This forces the reader to relate the ideas together, and question the reason behind the links. These occur on many levels: language (see **Language and style**); characters (see **Characters**); settings; events and themes.

 DID YOU KNOW?

Until the **Romantic** poets popularised mountain scenery, no one ever visited mountainous regions for pleasure.

The most obvious contrast is between indoor and outdoor settings. Characters often occupy enclosed spaces: Victor's 'workshop' at the top of his house, his dilapidated hut in the Orkneys, the prisons, the monster's hovel, Walton's cabin, and the barn Justine sleeps in. These can stand as **symbols** of mental as well as physical imprisonment. Characters are also seen as travelling over vast expanses of land. Most scenes outside are barren, wild, or desolate: the North Pole, the Mer de Glace, the peaks of the Alps, the Orkney islands. These often symbolise the separation of a character from his fellow beings. Notice that Clerval's enthusiasm for nature is as much produced by his own imagination as it is by the nature of the scenes themselves.

Journeys form a pattern in the narrative. Often the story moves in cycles. Characters separate from others and return to meet them under different circumstances. Most obvious is the way the monster keeps returning to meet Victor. This creates a haunting feeling. Victor travels away from his family many times and always returns to them under new pressures.

Chapters often 'mirror' each other in the book. Here are some examples:

- 1 and 11 are concerned with the childhood of Victor and the monster.

- 2 and 12 focus on the curious minds of Victor and the monster.

- 8 and 21 Victor finds himself in the same position as Justine.

- 5 and 20 show the difference in Victor's attitude to creating the two creatures.

- 10 and 17 either side of the monster's story, Victor and the monster argue and discuss his needs.

- 6 and 18 show the difference in Victor's spirits as he journeys with Clerval.

- 9 and 18 reveal Victor's solitude, self-absorption and guilt.

- 18 and 23 two female companions are destroyed but the tables are turned.

- 12 and 16 show how the monster's bright hopes turn to dark despair and revenge.

- 2 and 24 show how Victor's bright hopes have turned to dark despair and revenge.

Shelley uses this device to show either how characters have been changed by events, or how characters have not changed but are faced with a different situation.

CHARACTERS

We can learn about characters by looking at:

- Their actions, behaviour, and the way they speak

- Their desires, values, and concerns

- How they view other characters, situations and events

- How other characters view them and talk to them

- Their relationships with other characters

- What the writer tells us or suggests to us

CHECK THE BOOK

In her Introduction of 1831 to *Frankenstein* Mary Shelley writes of the nightmare that inspired the book: 'successive images ... arose ... the pale student of unhallowed arts kneeling beside the thing he had put together ... the hideous phantasm of a man ...'.

Ambitious
Imaginative
Impractical
Enthusiastic

ROBERT WALTON

Walton is the narrator who begins the novel. Victor Frankenstein is first seen through his eyes.

There is little physical description of Walton. This makes us focus on his emotional qualities, mental characteristics and the way he tells his story – his **voice**.

Walton is an important character who serves many literary purposes:

- His concerns set up the main themes and issues

- He is used to prompt the main tale and close it

- His obvious similarities to Victor make us look for important differences

Walton, an ambitious man of twenty-eight, is portrayed as emotionally volatile and unpredictable. The passionate and joyful way he opens the novel, when he tells us how he imagines the North Pole, is offset by his claim that 'his spirits are often depressed' (p. 15). Emotionally, too, his letters alternate between hope and gloom. Despite this, he is a determined character whose 'resolutions' are 'as fixed as fate' (p. 19). At the end, his need to succeed on his voyage blinkers his understanding of his crew's threat of mutiny.

Walton is depicted as a **Romantic** man. His strong imagination is a potential danger. His desire for exploration was first inspired by poems, books and childish fantasies. He is conscious that his 'daydreams' need to be controlled and yet appears incapable of controlling them himself (p. 18). This impractical sea-captain is prepared to sacrifice 'one man's life or death' in order to achieve his aims. His desires and ambitions prompt the main tale. The paths of Walton, Victor and the monster cross at the North Pole: it seems that this desolate **setting** is the only thing that can bring these unusual characters together. Walton's need for a friend and his uncontrollable desire for new knowledge provide the perfect triggers for Victor's tale which explores how these two things are essentially at odds.

Shelley carefully shows how Walton and Victor are similar. They like each other immediately and Walton begins to 'love him as a brother' (p. 26). Walton's prayers for a friend to regulate his mind seem to be answered with Victor, who is worried that Walton is pursuing the same course as he did in the past: Victor does not want Walton's desire for knowledge to be a 'serpent to sting' him (p. 28). Walton, therefore, appears to be presented with an image of his potential future self: a man wrecked and destroyed by his own ambition.

Both characters fail to realise the effect their actions can have on others. Walton's feeling that the mutiny is an 'injustice' mirrors the relationship between Victor and the monster. The crew becomes the rebellious monster of Walton's creation that stands up for its own rights. It is **ironic** that both characters feel themselves to be victims, yet both seem partially aware that their own 'mad schemes' are also to blame.

VICTOR FRANKENSTEIN

Victor is the second of the three narrators, and the central character of the novel.

Victor is loved by almost everyone: Caroline, Alphonse, Elizabeth, Ernest, Clerval, M. Krempe and M. Waldman, and even Mr Kirwin admire him. Walton introduces him as a 'celestial spirit', a 'divine wanderer', who has a 'never-failing power of judgment' (p. 28). Yet the reader knows these images only tell half the story. Either Mary Shelley was presenting us with a balanced view of Victor, or these **ironies** simply reveal the short-sightedness of her other characters.

The reader often feels **ambivalent** towards Victor. Like most tragic heroes, the traits of personality which make him a powerful character are the same traits which lead to his ruin.

We see early on that the combination of his 'thirst for knowledge' and his 'child's blindness' will be dangerous. We see the inner world of his mind blinding him to the realities of the outer world in Chapter 4, when his enthusiasm to discover the magnificent secrets of life lead to tamper with graveyards and dead bodies. Furthermore, he is so buried in his work, he fails to think of anything else: he forgets his family, abandons daylight, and does not

Passionate
Introverted
Imaginative
Enthusiastic
Single-minded

 **EXAMINER'S SECRET**
Collect quotations which illustrate emotional tension in Victor.

consider what he will do with his creation once it is brought to life. Despite these faults, the writing is so emotional and powerful, the reader is taken away with Victor on his imaginative journey and we also become 'exalted' (Chapters 3 and 4).

Victor seems either partially aware of his faults or unable to admit to them. His own ambition and passion for 'glory' are his worst enemies and he brings devastation upon himself. His inability to recognise this is seen by the way he blames outside influences such as his university teachers and the books he has read for his own downfall (Chapters 2 and 3). Although he emphasises that his own future was predestined, he hypocritically believes that Walton has the power to change his future by controlling his passion for knowledge.

Victor's self-contradictions become more frequent as his problems become deeper. He alternately blames himself and the monster for the deaths of William and Justine. Divided between feelings of guilt and revenge, he becomes at odds with himself. From Chapter 5, Victor is portrayed as a gloomy and lonely spirit whose need to keep the monster a secret creates an 'insurmountable barrier' (p. 153) between himself and those he loves. He has become the victim of his 'daemon'.

Our feelings towards Victor alter radically once we meet the monster: Victor should feel more remorse for abandoning the monster once he has created him. Victor's duty towards his family and humanity would have been better performed by doing his duty to the monster (Chapters 17 and 20). A female companion would remove the cause behind the monster's pain and quell his desire for revenge. However, our sympathy for the monster may lead us to underestimate the foulness of William's murder. It is understandable that Victor continues to see the monster as a 'devil' (Chapters 20 and 24).

Many of us may feel little pity for a character so wrapped up in himself. To us, it seems obvious that the monster's line 'I shall be with you on your wedding night' (p. 163) is a threat to kill Elizabeth. Yet Shelley makes it clear that Victor has not always thought of himself: after Justine's death, he draws near to Elizabeth 'lest at that very moment the destroyer had been near to rob me of her' (p. 89). Victor's self-absorption grows as a consequence of his genuine moral conflict (Chapters 18 and 19).

CHECK THE FILM

Gothic (1986), written and directed by Ken Russell, tells the story of the night Mary Shelley conceived her novel, with a star cast, including Natasha Richardson and Timothy Spall.

His death is truly tragic and **Romantic**. Despite all Victor's warnings against ambition, he still gives a rousing speech to the sailors, urging them on to meet the dangers of the ice, and also dies with the Romantic hope that another man might succeed in knowledge where he had failed. Although his desires have destroyed him, he cannot abandon his true character in the face of death.

ALPHONSE

Alphonse Frankenstein, Victor's father, is depicted as a kind, gentle and respectable man of wealth. His loyalty to his friend Beaufort is shown by his determination to seek him out and his willingness to give him money and assistance. Alphonse also finds a secure home for the orphaned Caroline, whom he eventually marries. Furthermore, Victor sees him as a good father who fulfilled his responsibilities as a parent with an 'active spirit of tenderness' (p. 32).

However, Victor's account is one-sided. Later, it emerges that Alphonse is a distant and formal man: by the tone of his reproachful letters, and the way he sends Victor away to university in another country, despite his son's grief for Caroline (Chapters 3 and 4).

Gentle
Respectable
Generous
Reproachful

As a father he is not approachable. Victor cannot confide his real problems in him. Alphonse is motivated by his selfish desire to see Victor and Elizabeth married quickly.

ELIZABETH

Victor introduces Elizabeth as a 'beautiful and adored companion' (p. 34). Her desire to create strong relationships with others is seen by her friendships with Victor and Clerval (Chapter 2) and by the way she plays a mother to Victor's younger brothers (Chapter 6). Her goodness is shown by her effect on others, she 'softens' the ambitions of Clerval and is able to 'subdue' Victor's violent temper. Although she is gentle, she is also courageous. Her speech in court defending Justine is needed because other witnesses refuse to come forward out of fear of being associated with a child-murderer.

Elizabeth is a forward-thinking woman who has democratic values. She is proud of being Genevan and is happy to see equality between the classes in Switzerland (p. 63). However, she is also naïve and idealistic. Her belief in human goodness is shattered by Justine's unjust execution. She realises that 'vice' is not 'imaginary' but real (p. 88).

Beautiful and good
Trusting and naïve

Hideous

Well meaning at first

Vengeful when thwarted

THE MONSTER

The monster is a gigantic eight-foot-tall creature who has been made from the parts of dead bodies. When he is brought to life Victor achieves the impossible. The monster's unnatural creation, his ugliness and power are reflected in Victor's first descriptions of him as a 'daemoniacal corpse' (p. 56) and a 'daemon'. Victor portrays him as other-worldly later when he sees him in the Alps coming towards him at 'superhuman speed' (p. 94). The monster's strength is seen in his physical endurance (Chapter 24). Shelley's use of **satanic imagery** to depict his emotions reveals him to be an evil character who should be feared. He appears to enjoy killing William and Elizabeth and is only satisfied when he reduces Victor to despair (Chapters 16, 23 and 24).

His merciless killing of Clerval, however, is the result of Victor's destruction of his half-finished female companion. The monster's fury and misery are the consequences of his loneliness and rejection by society. He begins life as an innocent and harmless being who has a natural attraction to humans. His child-like wonder and amazement at the world around him is beautiful and **Romantic** (Chapters 11 and 12). He loves nature, society and literature. He is a creature of good deeds: he collects wood for the De Laceys, saves a girl from drowning, and is a vegetarian!

His need for a friend is felt deeply. The brutal attacks on him by the villagers, Felix and the peasant who shoots him, make us pity him. The barrier between himself and humanity is his physical ugliness, nothing more. This is seen when De Lacey accepts him for what he is, a lonely being who needs understanding. His demand for a companion is his last hope and a justice which Victor finally denies. The way he is mistreated by humans turns him from a creature into a monster.

This imaginative and sensitive wanderer is essentially a Romantic hero. His hope for a female is denied him because of his tragic error in killing William and his envious framing of Justine, acts which he later despises. His final speeches are elevated and noble. The vision he has of his own suicide is exalted and **sublime** (Chapter 24).

WILLIAM

Although William is a minor character, he has a huge impact on the book as a whole. He is the youngest son of Alphonse Frankenstein and is murdered by the monster because he refuses to be his friend. His death serves many literary purposes:

Innocent
Beautiful

- It forces Victor to return home and encounter the monster on the way. His suspicion that the creature is the murderer raises expectations in the reader.

- It makes us sympathise with Victor. After overcoming the shock of the monster, this second misfortune follows quickly. His return to normal health is short-lived.

- It forms the basis of the subplot involving Justine. This allows Shelley to introduce political themes which are central to the relationship between Victor and the monster.

- The foulness of the murder makes Victor mistrust the monster. This mistrust makes him destroy the female creature.

- It shows how the monster is naïve in believing that William will be 'unprejudiced' (p. 137). Humans are prejudiced from an early age and this is the root of fear.

- It introduces the theme of mutual revenge between Victor and the monster.

DE LACEY

At the heart of the novel is a kind and gentle old blind man. He serves many literary purposes:

Warm-hearted
Poor
Blind
Forgiving

- His warm-hearted goodness to his family attract the monster who pins all his future hopes of happiness on befriending him.

- His poverty has not stopped him from loving his son, Felix, who is responsible for it. He is the only character who shows the capacity for forgiveness.

- The strong relationships he has created in his family emphasise the monster's loneliness and make the reader pity the creature.

- He is the only character in the book who shows the monster any kindness. His blindness prevents him from being prejudiced.

- The monster's desperation scares De Lacey and makes Felix misinterpret the monster's intentions.

MINOR CHARACTERS

Minor characters enable the author to:

- Move the plot forward
- Develop a theme
- Help us to learn more about the major characters

The novel is populated with a great number of minor characters who are used to mirror a quality of one, or more, of the major characters. This prompts the reader to question the difference between them. The minor characters can be grouped together.

Virtuous women

DID YOU KNOW?
Mary Shelley's mother wrote a book called *A Vindication of the Rights of Woman*.

Caroline Beaufort's kindness towards the poor is a 'passion' rather than a 'duty' (p. 33) because she remembered being the victim of poverty herself. Her adoption of the Elizabeth recalls her own history. Like Caroline, the orphans Elizabeth, Justine and Margaret all act as surrogate mothers. Agatha and Safie also show gentleness and kindness towards De Lacey and Felix. This kindness is precisely what the orphaned monster lacks.

Inadequate fathers

There are many fathers who, unlike the mothers, fail in their parental role. The fathers of Clerval, Walton, and Safie try to stop their children from pursuing their own interests. Their behaviour recalls Alphonse's dismissal of Victor's book. The Turk's tyrannical behaviour also mirrors Victor's attitude to the monster. Furthermore, the father of Elizabeth abandons her, and Caroline's father makes her suffer by his decision to hide from society after he lost his fortune. Their failures highlight Victor's more extreme failure to father the monster. All these fathers are different from De Lacey.

DID YOU KNOW?
Mary Shelley's father was called by Hugh Walpole, 'one of the greatest monsters exhibited by history'.

Ambitious sons

Felix, Clerval and Walton all have passionate ambitions to be benefactors to mankind in some way. The plans of Felix cause suffering to his family and Walton's plans have the potential to be fatal. Clerval's seem harmless because of Elizabeth's influence. While women appear to be preserving and creating human relationships, men seem to destroy them. Again, these characters mirror Victor's dangerous but well-meaning ambitions.

Scientists

We see three scientists other than Victor. The first is Alphonse's friend, who explains electricity and galvanism. These become ideas central to Victor's work. M. Waldman also has a huge influence on Victor because he explains the miracles of modern science. The other lecturer, M. Krempe, recalls Alphonse by his sarcastic dismissal of Victor's passion for alchemy.

Judges

It is **symbolic** that the only professional characters other than scientists are judges. This highlights the theme of how people judge each other and how the reader judges the characters. Although they are responsible for the well-being of others, only Mr Kirwin decides to seek actively for the real truth. The judges in Chapters 8 and 23 are portrayed as short-sighted.

Crowds

There are three crowds of people: the people who hear the trial of Justine, the Irish crowd who accuse Victor of murder, and the villagers who attack the monster. All are brutal, short-sighted and dangerous.

LANGUAGE AND STYLE

The novel has an interesting structure. In effect we are reading the correspondence between an explorer, Robert Walton, and his sister, Mrs Margaret Saville. Like bookends, the letters start and complete 'the tale' and its 'final and wonderful catastrophe' (p. 210). In Letter 2, Walton tells his sister 'I bitterly feel the want of a friend' (p. 17), someone with whom he can share his excitement of possible services to humanity: 'discovering a passage near to the pole' or 'ascertaining the secret of the magnet' (p. 14).

He rejoices when he strikes up the friendship with Victor Frankenstein, a man very similar to himself, one who also

? DID YOU KNOW?
The famous scientist, Humphry Davy, was a great friend of Mary Shelley's father.

sought 'knowledge and wisdom' (p. 28) and who offers Walton a story that he says might 'direct you if you succeed in your undertaking and console you in case of failure' (p. 29). We then hear two stories within the letters, the first from Frankenstein, the second from his creation, the monster.

It is interesting to note that Coleridge, one of Mary Shelley's important influences, said that a 'willing suspension of disbelief' (*Biographia Literaria*, 1817) is an essential ingredient of fantasy. We can see this in the ordinariness of the opening pages: an explorer looking to extend humanity's knowledge by venturing into the mysterious polar regions. It comes as no surprise when he meets Frankenstein and we, like sister Margaret, are led into a tale that starts plausibly enough – a man on a sledge drifting on 'a large fragment of ice' (p. 240). Our disbelief thus suspended, we read the story with mounting amazement!

DID YOU KNOW?

Coleridge said: 'Prose = words in their best order; – poetry = the *best* words in the best order'.

The author's choice of vocabulary and sentence structure gives a novel a particular flavour. This has a direct, if subconscious, impact on the reader's imagination and feelings.

An important idea in the novel is the double-sided nature of mankind: man is both great and horrid. We all experience the tension between good and evil in our characters. These contrasts are reflected in Shelley's language.

'THE LANGUAGE OF MY HEART'

Walton, Victor and the monster all adopt an emotional style of writing to describe their experiences. Their passions are always extreme. Shelley uses four main devices to show this.

Descriptive language

Shelley uses words which describe or are associated with feelings, such as the monster's 'tears of sorrow and delight'. She often uses adjectives and adverbs to intensify their feelings: phrases like 'eagerly longed', 'frantic impulse', and 'ardently desired' (p. 109) roll off the page.

Metaphors and similes

Shelley often compares her characters to other things. Walton sees Victor as a 'gallant vessel' who is 'wrecked'. Victor, famously, compares his passion for science to a 'mountain river' which 'swelling as it proceeded … became a torrent which, in its course, has swept away all my hopes and joys' (p. 37).

Contrasts

The three narrators have violent mood swings between joy and despair. We can find these contrasts by:

- Comparing two passages: Victor's fascination for science in Chapter 4 contrasts sharply to his reaction to Justine's trial in Chapter 8. His 'imagination' is 'exalted' and he is 'animated by an almost supernatural enthusiasm' (p. 49) for his work but he is filled with 'agony', 'sensations of horror' and 'heart-sickening despair' (pp. 81–2) when he realises its consequences.

- Looking for a contrast within a passage: when Walton talks with 'burning ardour' and becomes 'warmed' with the 'fervour' of his voyage the mood suddenly changes as a 'dark gloom spreads' over Victor's face and a 'groan burst' from him (p. 27).

- Looking for contrasts within a sentence or a phrase: Victor often uses this device to emphasise his reversal in fortune – 'misfortune had tainted my mind and changed its bright visions of extensive usefulness into gloomy and narrow reflections upon self' (p. 37).

Rhetorical language

Shelley uses repetition to build an emotional climax: Victor's mind is 'filled with one thought, one conception, one purpose' (p. 46). She also uses different types of sentences to create different moods. Walton's question to Margaret shows amazement: 'do you not feel your blood congeal with horror, like that which even curdles like mine?' (p. 202). Victor's exclamations, 'Abhorred monster! Fiend that thou art!' (p. 95) here adds emphasis to his insults.

 DID YOU KNOW?

When Mary Shelley wrote *Frankenstein* she set out to 'speak of the mysterious fears of our nature and awaken thrilling horror'.

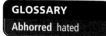

GLOSSARY

Abhorred hated

DID YOU KNOW?

Sir Walter Scott described *Frankenstein* as written in 'plain and forcible English' compared with the overblown language of other **Gothic novels** of the time.

KEY IMAGES

There are particular images which are repeated throughout the novel. These **motifs** recall another event and relate it to the present instance.

Hands

There are many times when characters cover their eyes with their hands when confronted with the monster. This image of refusing to see could suggest Victor's denial of his responsibilities, his blindness to the world around him, or his self-denial in accepting his own monstrosity.

We also see the image of the outstretched hand which is a **symbol** of the longing for human contact. Victor's need for his father is reciprocated whereas the monster's is not.

Finally we see hands as the agents of evil forces. Victor fails to shrink from his work as he 'dabbled among the unhallowed damps of the grave' (p. 52) but does so when he creates the female. Similarly, the monster's fingermarks on the necks of his victims are the dark evidence of strangulation – deeds which he later regrets.

Birth and death

Characters are 'restored to life' throughout, by the kind actions of other humans (see **Themes**). Shelley was aware of the contemporary scientific debates about a human life-force: many references are made to the human 'spirit' and 'animation'. These images contrast with the apparent death-in-life gloom of Victor who wanders 'like an evil spirit' (p. 86).

The moon and storms

The moon is strongly related to the presence of the monster. It appears when the monster is created and is also the first object in his world that gives him pleasure. It has a more eerie effect when it appears after the monster has promised revenge.

Storms occur frequently and create a sense of foreboding and chaos. They add to the tense **Gothic atmosphere**. These may be a **symbol** of the wild and chaotic emotions of the three main characters.

Books

Books populate the novel and have an important influence in determining the characters' destinies. This influence is bound up with the importance of the imagination (see **Themes**) – books affect us when we can see the images in our mind's eye. Uncle Tom's seafaring books and Coleridge are crucial for Walton, Agrippa for Victor, Milton for the monster, and ancient tales of chivalry for Clerval.

Windows

Windows or frame-like structures are symbols for a viewpoint on to reality (**see Themes**). They also symbolise a barrier between the characters either side of the window.

Heaven and hell

Images of light and dark, heaven and hell, warmth and cold, fire and ice, high and low, and joy and despair can be traced throughout. All these images recall *Paradise Lost*. Often, one of these pairs will tend to trigger off all the other pairs. The 'serpent' and the 'apple' which was 'already eaten' (p. 182) suggest that dark forces are at work, forces which will send the characters into despair.

IRONY

Shelley's use of **irony** and **dramatic irony** abound in the novel. She uses it to help the reader take a critical attitude towards the narrators. Shelley does not interfere directly with the narrative but calmly points out contradictions, denials and hypocrisies in her characters by using twists in the tale.

? DID YOU KNOW?
Lord Byron said of *Frankenstein*: 'Methinks it is a wonderful work for a girl of nineteen – *not* nineteen, indeed, at that time'.

Now, take a break!

PART FOUR

RESOURCES

HOW TO USE QUOTATIONS

One of the secrets of success in writing essays is the way you use quotations. There are five basic principles:

EXAMINER'S SECRET

Use quotations to support your answer.

❶ Put inverted commas at the beginning and end of the quotation.

❷ Write the quotation exactly as it appears in the original.

❸ Do not use a quotation that repeats what you have just written.

❹ Use the quotation so that it fits into your sentence.

❺ Keep the quotation as short as possible.

Quotations should be used to develop the line of thought in your essays.

Your comment should not duplicate what is in your quotation. For example:

EXAMINER'S SECRET

Keep your quotations as brief as possible.

> **Victor, in his struggle to decide whether to create the female mate for the creature, finally realises that he has no right to withhold happiness from him. He says, 'I had no right to withhold from him the small portion of happiness which was yet in my power to bestow.'**

Far more effective is to write:

> **Victor, in his struggle to decide whether to create the female mate for the creature, finally realises that he 'had no right to withhold from him the small portion of happiness' that was in his 'power to bestow'.**

However, the most sophisticated way of using the writer's words is to embed them into your sentence:

> **Victor, after having many doubts, finally realises that he has 'no right to withhold' the female mate from the creature and, in granting the creature's request, he would bestow the 'small portion of happiness' on him that is 'yet in his power'.**

When you use quotations in this way, you are demonstrating the ability to use text as evidence to support your ideas - not simply including words from the original to prove you have read it.

COURSEWORK ESSAY

Set aside an hour or so at the start of your work to plan what you have to do.

List all the points you feel are needed to cover the task. Collect page references of information and quotations that will support what you have to say. A helpful tool is the highlighter pen: this saves painstaking copying and enables you to target precisely what you want to use.

Focus on what you consider to be the main points of the essay. Try to sum up your argument in a single sentence, which could be the closing sentence of your essay. Depending on the essay title, it could be a statement about a character: The traits of Victor's personality which make him a powerful character are also those which lead to his ruin; an opinion about a setting: The frequent storms create a sense of foreboding and chaos; or a judgement on a theme: Walton, Victor and the monster all depict the world as an unknown mystery waiting to be discovered.

Make a short essay plan. Use the first paragraph to introduce the argument you wish to make. In the following paragraphs develop this argument with details, examples and other possible points of view. Sum up your argument in the last paragraph. Check you have answered the question.

Write the essay, remembering all the time the central point you are making.

On completion, go back over what you have written to eliminate careless errors and improve expression. Read it aloud to yourself, or, if you are feeling more confident, to a relative or friend.

If you can, try to type your essay, using a word processor. This will allow you to correct and improve your writing without spoiling its appearance.

EXAMINER'S SECRET

Examiners know the novel so they do not need to be told the story. Refer to aspects of the plot – do not write it out in detail.

SITTING THE EXAMINATION

Examination papers are carefully designed to give you the opportunity to do your best. Follow these handy hints for exam success:

EXAMINER'S SECRET

Read the entire exam paper before deciding which question to answer.

BEFORE YOU START

- Make sure you know the subject of the examination so that you are properly prepared and equipped.

- You need to be comfortable and free from distractions. Inform the invigilator if anything is off-putting, e.g. a shaky desk.

- Read the instructions, or rubric, on the front of the examination paper. You should know by now what you have to do but check to reassure yourself.

- Observe the time allocation – and follow it carefully. If they recommend 60 minutes for Question 1 and 30 minutes for Question 2, it is because Question 1 carries twice as many marks.

- Consider the mark allocation. You should write a longer response for 4 marks than for 2 marks.

WRITING YOUR RESPONSES

- Use the questions to structure your response, e.g. question: **'The endings of X's poems are always particularly significant. Explain their importance with reference to two poems.'** The first part of your answer will describe the ending of the first poem; the second part will look at the ending of the second poem; the third part will be an explanation of the significance of the two endings.

- Write a brief draft outline of your response.

- A typical 30-minute examination essay is probably between 400 and 600 words in length.

- Keep your writing legible and easy to read, using paragraphs to show the structure of your answers.

- Spend a couple of minutes afterwards quickly checking for obvious errors.

WHEN YOU HAVE FINISHED

- Don't be downhearted – if you found the examination difficult, it is probably because you really worked at the questions. Let's face it, they are not meant to be easy!

- Don't pay too much attention to what your friends have to say about the paper. Everyone's experience is different and no two people ever give the same answers.

IMPROVE YOUR GRADE

Your potential grades in any examination can always be improved. Every candidate everywhere starts at the same point: a blank answer booklet. An examiner marks your work according to a mark scheme that is applied to all candidates and no examiner knows in advance your level of achievement.

You must realise that the examination board has determined that your answer book contains more than enough space for any candidate to get the highest marks so there is no need to rush your writing in order to fill up three or four extra sheets!

Moreover, the examination board knows that the two hours that your examination is scheduled to last is enough for any candidate to secure the highest marks without rushing. You are not expected to write solidly for two hours since the examiner confidently believes that you will spend at least some of the time thinking!

So take your time. Think carefully, plan carefully, write carefully and check carefully. A relaxed performer always works best – in any field and in every examination!

Whatever you are studying, the way to be completely at ease with it in an examination is to know it inside out. There is no substitute for reading and re-reading the text.

The main reason that candidates let themselves down in the examination room is that they fail to read the question! Do not begin writing until you are quite sure what you want to say because it is very easy to lose track and end up writing off the

EXAMINER'S SECRET
Keep your handwriting neat and legible.

subject. Whilst you are writing, it is a good idea to check back occasionally to the question and satisfy yourself that you are still answering the question.

EXAMINER'S SECRET

There is no need to write reams; two to three sides for each essay are enough to get good marks!

Keep an eye on the clock. Most literature papers require you to answer two questions in two hours. It may seem obvious but it is worth reminding yourself that to do yourself justice you need to spend about an hour on each question! This is all the more important when you feel happier answering one question rather than the other. If you steal time to produce a lengthy answer on one question, you are far more likely to lose all the extra marks you have gained by handing in a feeble response for the question you did not like.

WHAT ARE EXAMINERS LOOKING FOR?

Let's look at ways that different candidates may *start* their responses to the question, 'Describe the importance of the trial of Justine in the novel?'

The D or E candidate will concentrate on literal evidence. S/he will give a simple description of the trial and offer simple statements in straightforward comments:

Justine is put on trial for the murder of William since they think she is confused because she must have done it. The family do not believe she is guilty since she loved William.

The father thinks it is not necessary to be upset because the law is just and if she is innocent she is bound to be cleared.

This is a very simple answer. The candidate will be rewarded for knowledge of the text but s/he would need to provide more comment supported by evidence quoted from the text if s/he wanted to gain higher marks.

The C or B candidate will pay more attention to the question, quoting from the book and attempting to offer some judgements:

The family are astonished when Justine is accused of the murder of William since they cannot believe that someone 'so amiable

EXAMINER'S SECRET

If you are asked to compare something, this means showing the differences and the similarities.

and fond of all the family could suddenly become capable of so frightful, so appalling a crime'.

The evidence against her consisted of a picture of the mother which was 'discovered in her pocket' and was taken to a magistrate who ordered her arrest.

Father is convinced that when she comes to trial, she will be acquitted since he feels that they can 'rely on the justice of (their) laws'. Victor, for his part, is relieved that since the case against her will have to rely upon 'circumstantial evidence', there will be insufficient to find her guilty.

This is a much better response than the literal description of the circumstances of the trial. The candidate is attempting to answer the question and using quotations to support the commentary. S/he attempts to explain the nature of the case against Justine and offers a personal comment. However, this sort of treatment is obviously going to result in a very long essay since the details of the case are being treated with such close consideration. A more focused answer will be achieved by rigorous planning of what family reactions to include.

The A or A* candidate assumes that the examiner knows the text. S/he will not spend time writing an account of the details of the crime and the trial but will concentrate on bringing out the writer's methods and the wider significance of this event in the novel as a whole. Such a candidate might open an essay thus:

The trial of Justine Moritz is the first illustraton of the dangers presented by the monster. From the outset we are perfectly aware from Alphonse's letter that William, the 'sweet child', has been murdered by the monster – the 'print of the murderer's finger ... on his neck' is a telling enough detail to establish the grisly facts. There is an immediate confession of guilt from a distraught Elizabeth which is quickly dismissed but the missing 'valuable miniature' may be the vital clue.

When this is discovered in the pocket of Justine, we know it is a compelling piece of circumstantial evidence which a simple jury might find hard to ignore but her protestations of innocence we feel should be enough to help the defence build up a convincing

EXAMINER'S SECRET
Finish early to check through what you have written.

EXAMINER'S SECRET
Read through what you have written. If you have forgotten to put in paragraphs, the examiner will understand if you write 'NP' in the margin.

case. When she changes her plea, we are mystified but her explanation of the violence towards her of her 'confessor' who 'threatened excommunication and hell fire' reassures us of her innocence. Yet again the author had provided us with a character whose innocence is plain yet who is condemned by all around her on a single piece of circumstantial evidence. The haste to secure justice without due consideration is a feature of the novel, and we see it used against the monster himself, as for instance when he saves a little girl from drowning, only to be accused of attempting to murder her himself.

This response shows the ability to integrate comment, description and reference. The quotations show that the writer has fully absorbed what is written into his or her own thinking.

There is no attempt here to write a blow-by-blow account of the crime and the trial: the candidate has a view of the whole visit and the response ranges comfortably across a wide section of the novel.

There is a real attempt to be precise by careful choise of vocabulary: 'a compelling piece of circumstantial evidence', 'a telling enough detail', 'the haste to secure justice without due consideration'. The writer is also trying to draw a wider point from what s/he has read: that the trial illustrates how miscarriages of justice occur here as elsewhere in the novel and thus shows exactly why the trial of Justine has a wider importance in the novel.

SAMPLE ESSAY PLAN

A typical essay question on *Frankenstein* is followed by a sample essay plan in note form. This does not present the only answer to the question, so do not be afraid to include your own ideas, or exclude some of the following. Remember that quotations are essential to prove and illustrate the points you make.

In what ways does Mary Shelley make you sympathise with the monster?

EXAMINER'S SECRET
Everything you write is marked, even what you have crossed out. You may accidentally have crossed out something worth extra marks.

INTRODUCTION

Analyse the key elements of the question. The 'ways' of the question involve looking at Shelley's literary techniques, and the impact of these in creating pity for the monster. The monster is a complex character: his violent and cruel actions shock us but these actions are counterbalanced with kind actions.

PART 1

The monster is portrayed as an evil force in Chapters 5 and 7. These fearful expectations are developed by making him the suspect for William's murder. Justine's death is a consequence of the murder. The way she suffers and the despair that Victor and his family are put through shows the monster's capability for destruction.

PART 2

Our initial view of the monster is radically challenged and our sympathy for Victor undermined. Note our surprise at his speeches in Chapter 10. The monster's attempt at evoking sympathy is balanced by Victor's scepticism. Is the monster just a persuasive speaker who is hiding evil intentions? Explain how the monster is portrayed as a harmless, child-like and vulnerable being in Chapters 11 and 12. Notice how the loneliness and abandonment of the monster make us read back and re-evaluate Victor's behaviour in Chapter 5.

The author's use of the monster as a narrator influences our feelings about him: we see things from the monster's viewpoint and we become involved with his feelings. We pity him when he sees himself in the pool: it is Victor who is responsible for his ugliness. Characters hate him for his ugliness and do not give him a chance to show what he is really like – a good and sensitive being who needs a friend.

PART 3

Look at how the structure is important. It is a turning point when Felix beats him, after he has become emotionally involved in the lives of the De Laceys. Explain that his growing sensitivity to the world around him and what he reads makes him self-conscious of his difference. He puts all his hopes on the De Laceys. Their departure thwarts his plans.

EXAMINER'S SECRET
If your question contains bullet points covering topics relevant to your answer, use them to help structure your response.

PART 4

Victor Frankenstein becomes the focus of our anger in Chapter 16. Notice Shelley's cleverness when William is murdered: we feel more sympathy for the monster because William is portrayed as yet another prejudiced human! Explain how the monster's actions can be partially 'excused' because of the way humans have treated him. Emphasise the logic and justice of the monster's demands.

EXAMINER'S SECRET

The best candidates make cross-references, showing the connections between different parts of the novel.

PART 5

Explain how Shelley uses characters to develop themes. Show how the monster's concerns relate to other characters. Explore how Shelley is concerned with imprisonment, prejudice, justice, and the duty of parents. Contrast how the orphans Caroline, Elizabeth and Walton have been accepted. Contrast how Safie, despite her cultural differences is accepted by the De Laceys. Contrast Victor's childhood with the monster's. Contrast Victor's friends Clerval and Elizabeth with the monster's lack of friends. Show how the monster can be seen as an innocent, outcast victim.

PART 6

As the story is finally unfolded, the reader's sympathies become split between Victor and the monster. Victor's delays in creating the female cause tension. We have divided feelings when he destroys her; conflicting sympathies when the monster, out of revenge, plunges Victor into desolation. We see that the monster wants to make him suffer the same things he has suffered, yet this will not solve anything. Show how these actions really do turn him into a devilish monster.

CONCLUSION

Show your final opinion of the question. We are shown the innocence of the monster's childhood and this undermines our initial impressions of him. Shelley's narrative technique, the contrasts between him and the other characters, and depiction of the monster as a noble being make us have more sympathy for him than Victor. Her use of irony reveals Victor's essential lack of awareness and his dying comments show how little he has learned. Compare this with the final encounter between the monster and Walton and show the impact this has upon our sympathy.

FURTHER QUESTIONS

Make a plan as shown and attempt these questions:

1 How much sympathy does the writer make you have for Victor Frankenstein?

2 Examine the differences between the male and female characters in the novel.

3 The relationship between Victor and the monster is important to the novel. Trace the development of this relationship as the novel progresses, analysing the main points in its development.

4 What do you find interesting about Shelley's use of locations and nature in the novel? How does this enhance our understanding of the whole novel?

5 Explain how each of the major characters in the novel, Walton, Victor and the monster, is important to our understanding of what the novel is about.

6 In what ways is *Frankenstein* a book of the emotions and the imagination?

7 To what extent is Victor Frankenstein responsible for his own downfall? How does this link with the decline of the monster?

8 If you were Victor Frankenstein, would you create the female creature for the monster? Discuss the reasons behind your decision in detail.

9 How reliable, in your opinion, is Victor Frankenstein as a storyteller? You should consider his attitude and behaviour towards the monster, the effect of the monster's story on the reader, and Walton's confrontation with the monster.

10 Discuss Shelley's portrayal of the nature of good and evil and of the conflict of these forces in man's personality.

EXAMINER'S SECRET
Keep checking on the wording of the question as you write. This will stop you drifting off the point.

LITERARY TERMS

ambivalence when an author or character feels two opposite extremes of emotion at the same time

atmosphere a setting or situation's mood

Byronic the qualities pertaining to the rebellious heroes created by the poet, Lord Byron. They are usually gloomy, proud and disdainful but also mysterious, attractive and magnetic

chinese-box narration when an author wraps a story inside a story inside another story you could liken this to a chinese box

Enlightenment in eighteenth-century France, a time when philosophers were convinced that the application of Reason would solve the problems of humanity. Reason was thought to lead naturally to scientific discovery. Mary Shelley's father, William Godwin, was a disciple of this intellectual movement

epic a long narrative poem, written in elevated style about the exploits of superhuman heroes

fantasy a kind of imagining, divorced from any contact with the real world of things and ideas

feminism a political movement which fights for women's equality and freedom from social and economic dependency upon men

flashback when the narration jumps backward in time to an earlier point in the story

genre a type or class of literature which follows the same form, e.g., horror, science-fiction, realism, spy-thriller

Gothic novel an influential literary genre that contains supernatural, unexplained and weird events in order to provoke either terror or horror in the reader. Its imagery is usually inspired by dreams and nightmares. It flourished 1765–1900, and, at the time, was far more popular than realism

imagery any language which requires the reader to form a mental picture

implied meaning the meaning beneath the surface

irony a 'tongue in cheek' piece of language where the meaning beneath the surface is in contrast with the apparent meaning. It is usually used so the author can make a subtle criticism of a character without intruding directly and obtrusively into the text. The effect can be either humorous, serious, or both. **dramatic irony** is when the audience or reader is aware of something the character is not

metaphor when two things are compared implicitly, e.g., Frankenstein is a 'gallant vessel' to Cpt Walton

motif an image, idea, or situation which recurs throughout the text forming a pattern, e.g., the association between the monster and the moon

multiple narration when a story is told using more than one narrator

multiple viewpoint when a story is told from the perspective of more than one character

narrator the story-teller

paradox when language or a state of affairs seems to contradict itself on the surface but makes sense underneath, e.g., it is paradoxical that the monster hates Frankenstein but cannot do without him

realism writing which deals in a down-to-earth way with ordinary life

rhetorical question a question that is asked in order to emphasise a point rather than expect an answer

Romantic an influential cultural movement in literature, music and painting (in the late eighteenth and early nineteenth centuries) that focused on the expression of sublime emotions aroused by nature, the imagination, dreams and solitude. Romantics include Byron, Turner, Blake, Wordsworth, Coleridge, the Shelleys and Keats, in Britain; and Beethoven, Schiller, Hoffmann and Goethe in Germany

satanic school the Romantic poets William Blake, Percy Shelley and Lord Byron thought that the character of Satan in *Paradise Lost* by John Milton should be seen as an attractive and justified rebel who was fighting against a tyrannical God for his own freedom

science-fiction an influential literary genre which concentrates on the way technological progress can and does affect mankind. Stories are often set in the future and have disastrous outcomes

setting the place or environment where the events in a story are set. Settings are sometimes used to create a mood, reflect a character's inner feelings, or used symbolically

simile when two things are compared by using the word 'like' or 'as'

sublime refers to a stimulus which arouses exalted emotions; it may be a feeling of overpowering joy or, alternatively, terror

symbolism when one image is used to mean something else, often an idea or emotion

uncanny an eerie feeling created by something seemingly supernatural

CHECKPOINT HINTS/ANSWERS

CHECKPOINT 1 He believes it is 'a region of beauty and delight'. (p. 13)

CHECKPOINT 2 His men are 'bold and apparently firm of purpose'. (p. 21)

CHECKPOINT 3 He admires him: Victor has 'extraordinary merits' and is a 'wonderful man'. (p. 28)

CHECKPOINT 4 He was the father of Caroline, Victor's mother.

CHECKPOINT 5 Waldman thinks Victor has 'ability' and he has 'no doubt of (his) success'. (p. 47)

CHECKPOINT 6 Victor quotes lines from Coleridge's *Rime of the Ancient Mariner*. (p. 57)

CHECKPOINT 7 Justine is looked upon almost as a member of the family. (p. 63)

CHECKPOINT 8 He initially believes she is guilty but changes his mind once Victor assures him otherwise and then hopes for her acquittal. (p. 76)

CHECKPOINT 9 They are enraged and feel Justine is guilty of 'the blackest ingratitude'. (p. 81)

CHECKPOINT 10 He feels he 'ought to render him happy before (he) complained of his wickedness'. (p. 97)

CHECKPOINT 11 The kindness he shows towards 'his children' as he called them. (p. 108)

CHECKPOINT 12 She is very beautiful. (p. 112)

CHECKPOINT 13 She takes money and jewels and escapes from her father. (p. 122)

CHECKPOINT 14 He finds Victor's papers in the pockets of a laboratory coat. (p. 125)

CHECKPOINT 15 His feelings of 'kindness and gentleness' are changed to a 'hellish rage' when he is shot at. (p. 136)

CHECKPOINT 16 He says that it will make him happy to see that he can 'excite the sympathy of some living thing'. (p. 141)

CHECKPOINT 17 As a father, he is keen that Victor should have a companion. (p. 148)

CHECKPOINT 18 After disposing of the female monster, he falls asleep and is taken by the sea. (p. 166)

CHECKPOINT 19 He had been strangled: there was 'the black mark of fingers on his neck'. (p. 169)

CHECKPOINT 20 He says that it would be impossible to follow 'an animal which can traverse the sea of ice'. (p. 193)

TEST YOURSELF (LETTERS 1–4)

1 Walton (p. 17)

2 Victor (p. 27)

3 Walton (p. 14)

4 Victor (p. 25)

5 Walton (p. 26)

6 The monster (p. 23)

7 Victor (p. 24)

8 Walton (p. 25)

9 Margaret (p. 18)

10 Victor (p. 26)

TEST YOURSELF (CHAPTERS 1–5)

1 Alphonse (p. 37)

2 Waldman (p. 46)

3 Victor (p. 53)

4 Victor (p. 54)

5 Coleridge (p. 57)

6 Elizabeth (p. 36)

7 Clerval (p. 36)

8 The monster (p. 56)

9 Victor (p. 58)

10 Clerval (p. 60)

TEST YOURSELF (CHAPTERS 6-10)

1 Victor (p. 86)

2 Elizabeth (p. 88)

3 The monster (p. 96)

4 The monster (p.96)

5 Justine (p. 83)

6 Elizabeth (p. 75)

7 Justine (p. 79)

8 Justine's mother (p. 64)

9 William and Justine (p. 85)

10 Elizabeth (p. 87)

TEST YOURSELF (CHAPTERS 11-16)

1 The monster (p. 142)

2 De Lacey (p. 129)

3 The monster (p.124)

4 William (p.137)

5 The monster (p. 138)

6 Justine (p. 138)

7 Safie (p. 122)

8 William (p. 137)

9 Felix (p. 104)

10 The De Laceys (p. 130)

TEST ANSWERS

Margaret Atwood
Cat's Eye
The Handmaid's Tale

Jane Austen
Emma
Mansfield Park
Persuasion
Pride and Prejudice
Sense and Sensibility

Alan Bennett
Talking Heads

William Blake
Songs of Innocence and of Experience

Charlotte Brontë
Jane Eyre
Villette

Emily Brontë
Wuthering Heights

Angela Carter
Nights at the Circus

Geoffrey Chaucer
The Franklin's Prologue and Tale
The Miller's Prologue and Tale
The Prologue to the Canterbury Tales
The Wife of Bath's Prologue and Tale

Samuel Coleridge
Selected Poems

Joseph Conrad
Heart of Darkness

Daniel Defoe
Moll Flanders

Charles Dickens
Bleak House
Great Expectations
Hard Times

Emily Dickinson
Selected Poems

John Donne
Selected Poems

Carol Ann Duffy
Selected Poems

George Eliot
Middlemarch
The Mill on the Floss

T.S. Eliot
Selected Poems
The Waste Land

F. Scott Fitzgerald
The Great Gatsby

E.M. Forster
A Passage to India

Brian Friel
Translations

Thomas Hardy
Jude the Obscure
The Mayor of Casterbridge
The Return of the Native
Selected Poems
Tess of the d'Urbervilles

Seamus Heaney
Selected Poems from 'Opened Ground'

Nathaniel Hawthorne
The Scarlet Letter

Homer
The Iliad
The Odyssey

Aldous Huxley
Brave New World

Kazuo Ishiguro
The Remains of the Day

Ben Jonson
The Alchemist

James Joyce
Dubliners

John Keats
Selected Poems

Christopher Marlowe
Doctor Faustus
Edward II

Arthur Miller
Death of a Salesman

John Milton
Paradise Lost Books I & II

Toni Morrison
Beloved

George Orwell
Nineteen Eighty-Four

Sylvia Plath
Selected Poems

Alexander Pope
Rape of the Lock & Selected Poems

William Shakespeare
Antony and Cleopatra
As You Like It
Hamlet
Henry IV Part I
King Lear
Macbeth
Measure for Measure
The Merchant of Venice
A Midsummer Night's Dream
Much Ado About Nothing
Othello
Richard II
Richard III
Romeo and Juliet
The Taming of the Shrew
The Tempest
Twelfth Night
The Winter's Tale

George Bernard Shaw
Saint Joan

Mary Shelley
Frankenstein

Jonathan Swift
Gulliver's Travels and A Modest Proposal

Alfred Tennyson
Selected Poems

Virgil
The Aeneid

Alice Walker
The Color Purple

Oscar Wilde
The Importance of Being Earnest

Tennessee Williams
A Streetcar Named Desire

Jeanette Winterson
Oranges Are Not the Only Fruit

John Webster
The Duchess of Malfi

Virginia Woolf
To the Lighthouse

W.B. Yeats
Selected Poems

Metaphysical Poets

THE ULTIMATE WEB SITE FOR THE ULTIMATE LITERATURE GUIDES

At York Notes we believe in helping you achieve exam success. Log on to **www.yorknotes.com** and see how we have made revision even easier, with over 300 titles available to download twenty-four hours a day. The downloads have lots of additional features such as pop-up boxes providing instant glossary definitions, user-friendly links to every part of the guide, and scanned illustrations offering visual appeal. All you need to do is log on to **www.yorknotes.com** and download the books you need to help you achieve exam success.

KEY FEATURES:

Details on how York Notes can help you

Menu Bar to help you find your way around the site

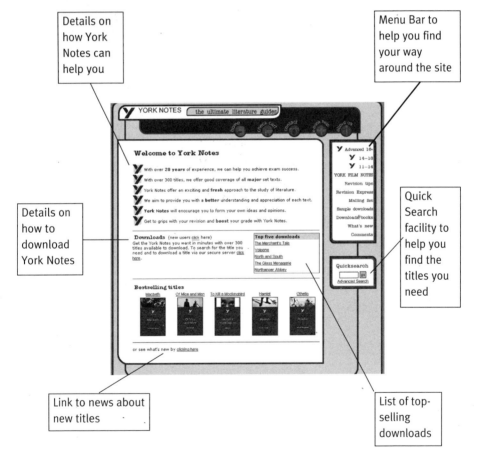

Details on how to download York Notes

Quick Search facility to help you find the titles you need

Link to news about new titles

List of top-selling downloads